HOCKEY'S GREATEST STARS

THIRD EDITION

HOCKEY'S GREATEST STARS

THIRD EDITION

LEGENDS AND YOUNG LIONS

Chris McDonell

FIREFLY BOOKS

A FIREFLY BOOK

Published by Firefly Books Ltd. 2011
Copyright © 2011 Firefly Books Ltd.

Text copyright © 2011 Chris McDonell
Images copyright © as listed on page 187

First printing

Publisher Cataloging-in-Publication Data (U.S.)
McDonell, Chris.
    Hockey's greatest stars : legends and young lions / Chris McDonell.
3rd ed.
[192] p. : photos. (chiefly col.) ;   cm.
Includes bibliographical references and index.
Summary: Profiles of the greatest National Hockey League players of all time plus
those who are current players.
ISBN 978-1-55407-888-2   (pbk.)
1. Hockey players -- Biography. 2. National Hockey League. I. Title.
796.962/0922 B dc22   GV848.5.A1M336 2011

Library and Archives Canada Cataloguing in Publication
McDonell, Chris, 1960-
    Hockey's greatest stars : legends and young
lions / Chris McDonell. -- 3rd ed.
Includes bibliographical references and index.
ISBN 978-1-55407-888-2
    1. Hockey players--Canada--Biography. 2. Hockey players--Biography.
3. National Hockey League--Biography. I. Title.
GV848.5.A1M26 2011   796.962092'2   C2011-903670-3

Published in the United States by
Firefly Books (U.S.) Inc.
P.O. Box 1338, Ellicott Station
Buffalo, New York 14205

Published in Canada by
Firefly Books Ltd.
66 Leek Crescent
Richmond Hill, Ontario L4B 1H1

Cover and interior design: Kimberley Young

Printed in Canada

*The Publisher gratefully acknowledges the financial support for our publishing program by the Government of
Canada through the Canada Book Fund as administered by the Department of Canadian Heritage.*

CONTENTS

Introduction............................ 8

CENTERS

Legends......................... 10
Lions 42

WINGERS

Legends......................... 54
Lions 86

DEFENSEMEN

Legends......................... 98
Lions 130

GOALTENDERS

Legends......................... 142
Lions 174

Acknowledgements 186
Photo Credits.........................187
Bibliography 188
Index 189

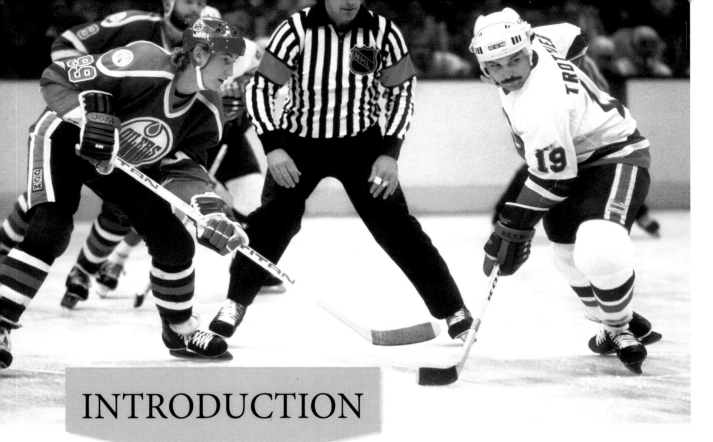

INTRODUCTION

"I respected 'Rocket' Richard," Gordie Howe once said, "but I didn't like him. He was the man who led the way for the rest of us. He was my pacemaker — first for career points, then for career goals."

And so it follows that stars beget stars: from Richard to Howe to Bobby Orr to Wayne Gretzky to Mario Lemieux to Alex Ovechkin to Sidney Crosby — the list is ever growing, and on it are the finest players to ever play the game.

Hockey's Greatest Stars profiles the best of these players: the "legends" (the greatest players of all time) and the "young lions" (players who are prowling the NHL arenas — all were born in 1984 or later). There were many worthy candidates, and it was an arduous task to select only 60 of the best players who ever laced up skates. It wasn't any easier to pick the top-20 young stars of today. When it came down to it, looking at statistics and accumulated awards was instructive, but it was not enough.

Statistics from different eras cannot be compared in a completely straightforward manner. A second assist was rarely given on goals during Charlie Conacher's career in the 1930s; Georges Vezina, who died in 1926 and for whom the NHL's best goaltender award is named, never played a game in which the rules permitted a netminder to hold or smother the puck. It is an oft-repeated maxim that the best players would star in any era; yet as Nels Stewart commented, even the renowned Howie Morenz would have had a difficult time in the NHL of the 1950s.

Another important ingredient in the makeup of a great hockey player is his contribution to team success. "Steve Yzerman is the best example," said winger Brendan Shanahan about Yzerman's ability to transform himself from a prolific scorer to a shut-down centerman. "He's a guy whose image has gone back and forth so many times in the [Detroit] organization, and now he's considered one of the greatest captains to ever play. That's what winning does for all of us."

Strong performance under playoff pressure

lifted many into *Hockey's Greatest Stars*, although the lack of a Stanley Cup ring was never a reason for exclusion. "I have been able to maintain my scoring pace while guys like Guy Lafleur have tailed off," Marcel Dionne once remarked with a wistful smile. "I always get an extra two months of rest because we never make the playoffs." Among the legends in these pages are some who never hoisted the Cup. And goaltender Vladislav Tretiak didn't even compete in the NHL.

Beyond choosing the players, I made no attempt to rank them. In the end, it came down to singular decisions — this star or that? — and the answers were never easy. Consistency and durability were given more weight than meteoric exploits for the legends' roster, less so for the young lions. Thus, a player such as 700-goal-scorer Mike Gartner is included, while 1972 Team Canada hero Paul Henderson did not make the cut. Several other players might have joined Gartner in this book had they put in more years as consistently as he did — winger Pavel Bure springs immediately to mind. Likewise, it

was hard to exclude players such as goaltender Tony Esposito, a frequent All-Star during his lengthy career with the Chicago Black Hawks. Yet when everything was factored in, center Phil is the only Esposito on this honor roll.

The results of these difficult decisions are now before you. After perusing the table of contents, try to put aside your own arguments for a while. The portraits offered here, in words and pictures, sketch talented, gritty and inspiring men who represent all that is wonderful and exciting about the fabulous sport of hockey. The game itself has its own charm, but the players bring it to life.

As Gretzky observed at the 1999 All-Star Game, "One of the greatest parts of our game is the history.... There are some guys who don't get as much recognition as they deserve for getting hockey to the level it is today." From Morenz to Richard to Howe to Gretzky to the young lions of today, these vignettes, although arranged by position rather than in chronological order, collectively serve as a snapshot of all that is hockey — past, present and future.

CENTERS

LEGENDS

Syl Apps 12

Jean Beliveau 14

Bobby Clarke 16

Marcel Dionne 18

Phil Esposito 20

Wayne Gretzky 22

Mario Lemieux 24

Mark Messier 26

Stan Mikita 28

Howie Morenz 30

Henri Richard 32

Milt Schmidt 34

Nels Stewart 36

Bryan Trottier 38

Steve Yzerman 40

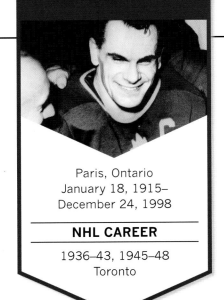

Paris, Ontario
January 18, 1915–
December 24, 1998

NHL CAREER

1936–43, 1945–48
Toronto

SYL APPS

Syl Apps combined Boy Scout virtue with exceptional athletic ability — the perfect profile for a hockey hero. Although Apps had only a 10-season career, he is still regarded as one of the greatest captains the Toronto Maple Leafs ever had. His minuscule 56 career penalty minutes attest to his sportsmanship, but his chiseled good looks, great physical strength and slick stickhandling, passing and scoring were equally important to the lasting image he created.

Apps helped the Maple Leafs win three Stanley Cups, captained the team after his World War II service and quit the game while still at his peak. An all-round athlete who excelled at hockey, football and track, Apps was the 1934 Commonwealth Games pole vault champion and delayed accepting Conn Smythe's invitation to join the Maple Leafs so that he could compete in the 1936 Olympics.

He went on to win the inaugural Calder Trophy in 1937, but the spring of 1942 provided his greatest excitement. "Nothing can compare," he said, "with the thrill of winning our fourth in a row over the Red Wings after they had won three straight." No other team has ever made such an amazing comeback in the Stanley Cup final. "If you want to pin me down to not only

my biggest night in hockey but also my biggest second," he told writer Trent Frayne in 1949, "I'll say it was the last tick of the clock that sounded the final bell. I'll never forget it."

Halfway through the 1942–43 season, Apps broke his leg and shocked Leafs owner Conn Smythe when he tried to return part of his salary — he felt he hadn't earned his full pay. Once the leg healed, he volunteered for Canadian military service, missing two full NHL seasons at the height of his career.

Apps picked up right where he had left off when he returned from the war. In 1947, Hockey Hall of Fame–defenseman Bill Quackenbush claimed that Apps was the hardest player in the league to stop. "When he hits the defense," said Quackenbush, "he doesn't slow down, he digs in. That extra burst of speed makes him awful tough." Apps, however, believed he had lost a step. He wanted to retire before he "slowed the team down," but he set one last target: 200 career goals.

Heading into the final weekend of play in the spring of 1948, Apps needed only three more goals to reach 200. He scored one on Saturday night. In Sunday's game against Detroit, he banged in another one after a goalmouth scramble in the second period. Later in the

STATS:

	GP	G	A	Pts	PIM
RS	423	201	231	432	56
PO	69	25	29	54	8

same period, his teammate Harry Watson had an excellent scoring opportunity, but instead of shooting he passed to Apps, who scored goal 200. "I just blasted it with everything I had," said Apps. He put the icing on the cake by completing a hat trick in the third period.

The press commented on how generous Watson had been in setting Apps up for the goal. "It was nice of him all right," agreed Apps, "but you should have heard the yelling I was doing at him to pass it!" Apps hoisted the Stanley Cup for the second consecutive year, but when the Maple Leafs won their third straight championship the following season, it was without Apps in the lineup. The 33-year-old captain had retired and joined the business world.

"I was always keen about politics," explained Apps, when he answered yet another calling years later. He was elected as a member of the governing Progressive Conservative Party in 1963, and his image was untarnished by 11 years in Ontario politics. True to form, he retired on his own terms in 1974.

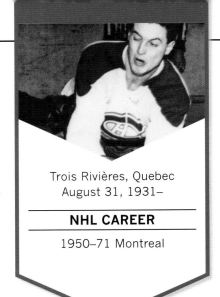

Trois Rivières, Quebec
August 31, 1931–

NHL CAREER

1950–71 Montreal

JEAN BELIVEAU

No one meeting Jean Beliveau today would be surprised to hear that he was offered an appointment to the Canadian Senate as well as the prestigious position of Governor General of Canada, as during his 20-year NHL hockey career, Beliveau was every bit the diplomat. Although he was never a recipient of the Lady Byng Trophy, Beliveau was hockey's greatest gentleman and a born leader. Upon Maurice "Rocket" Richard's retirement from the Montreal Canadiens in 1960, Beliveau quickly became the quintessential team captain.

James Christie of the *Globe and Mail* recorded Beliveau's own reflections on leadership: "To me, there are three things that a captain should do. First is what the fans see during a game. There is your play and the job you do as the man in the middle, the man between the coaches and the players and the referee. Second, there is the job every day in the dressing room. You have to listen to your teammates, even help them with their personal problems. I always tried to solve things right there in the dressing room, without going to management. Third, especially with the Canadiens, you act as a spokesman and representative wherever you go. But the most important of these is number two. You have to be ready to give time to your teammates in any

situation." Both on and off the ice, "Le Gros Bill" earned undying respect.

Few players have entered the NHL with as much fanfare as Beliveau did. The Canadiens wooed him unsuccessfully for years. Beliveau's patience paid off: By the time he signed with Montreal at age 22, he was one of the highest-paid players in the NHL. His first contract paid $105,000 over five years, plus bonuses — an astronomical sum in 1953. But Beliveau had been making similar money with the Quebec Aces in the Quebec Hockey League, and it took more than cash to get him into the NHL.

Beliveau played as a junior for two years in Quebec City with the Citadels and was honored with his first "Jean Beliveau Night" in 1951. The whole city had embraced the 61-goal scorer (in a 43-game season). Although Montreal beckoned, Beliveau decided to stay in Quebec City. In an ostensibly amateur league, Beliveau earned a then-enormous $15,000 a year, and he reciprocated with 45- and 50-goal seasons. Meanwhile, he had already signed a contract with Montreal stipulating that he would play for the Canadiens when he turned professional.

Beliveau had played two NHL games in 1950–51, getting a goal and an assist, and he donned the famous *bleu, blanc et rouge* sweater for three games in the 1952–53 season, scoring five times. The Canadiens took drastic action: They bought the entire Quebec senior league and made it officially professional. Beliveau's hand was forced, and at the start of the 1953–54 season, he began his much-anticipated rookie campaign.

Unfortunately, Beliveau struggled at the outset, was injured and finished with an unimpressive 13 goals and 21 assists in 44 games. Montreal's perseverance was rewarded in his second season (37 goals, 36 assists) and even more so in his third season. "I used to wonder why 'Rocket' Richard would blow up when other players chopped at

him," Beliveau said in 1956, "but I am beginning to understand." Responding to critics who urged him to use his size and strength to better advantage, Beliveau adopted a more belligerent style, albeit temporarily. His 143 penalty minutes in 1955–56 set a team record, but, more importantly, his 47 goals and 41 assists led the league. He scored 12 more goals in Montreal's 10-game march to Stanley Cup victory, the first of five consecutive winning seasons.

Although Beliveau failed to win another scoring title, the goals came regularly over the years. On February 11, 1971, during his final NHL season, he became only the fourth player to record 500 career goals. He capped his glorious career by hoisting the Stanley Cup for a 10th time.

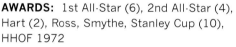

AWARDS: 1st All-Star (6), 2nd All-Star (4), Hart (2), Ross, Smythe, Stanley Cup (10), HHOF 1972

STATS:

	GP	G	A	Pts	PIM
RS	1,125	507	712	1,219	1,029
PO	162	79	97	176	211

Flin Flon, Manitoba
August 13, 1949–

NHL CAREER

1969–84 Philadelphia

BOBBY CLARKE

One of hockey's greatest leaders and one of its dirtiest players, Bobby Clarke earned both tags. Each characterization was intrinsic to Clarke's role in the 1970s as captain of Philadelphia's infamous "Broad Street Bullies," a team that constantly tried to blur the line between aggression and violence. Red Kelly, then coach of the Toronto Maple Leafs, added an important nuance: "I don't think I'd call Clarke dirty — mean is a better word."

"Guys who complain about my being dirty," countered Clarke, "should go home with my body at night. I've eaten quite a few too." (Sticks, that is.) Clarke's toothless grin has become one of hockey's enduring images, and it is still used to sell the game (and beer) almost 40 years after he led Philadelphia to its first of two consecutive Stanley Cups in 1974.

Clarke showed early promise as a hockey player in Flin Flon, Manitoba, but at the age of 15 he'd arrived at a crossroads. Diagnosed with juvenile diabetes, Clarke began self-administering the daily insulin injections he needed to stay healthy. Medical advice confirmed his conviction that his diabetes need not end his dream of playing professional hockey, and by the time Clarke was 17, he was starring in Jr. A hockey for the Flin Flon Bombers in what is now the Western Hockey League (WHL). Working in the mines a few hours each day further hardened his resolve to make hockey his career.

Clarke entered the 1969 NHL entry draft ranked the premier player in the WHL, but many questioned whether he could sustain the NHL pace. The Philadelphia Flyers took a chance on him with their second pick, drafting him 17th overall. It was the best move the franchise ever made.

Clarke fainted after his first shift in training camp, but it was soon determined that his diet simply needed to be adjusted, and he had a decent 1969–70 rookie season. His growing success and perseverance were acknowledged with the Bill Masterton Trophy in 1972. Later that fall, Clarke played a big role in Team Canada's narrow victory over the Soviet Union. Clarke's tenacious checking was invaluable, but his vicious two-handed slash on the ankle of Soviet star Valeri Kharlamov is what is best remembered. The intentional foul forced Kharlamov out of one game entirely and severely limited his effectiveness in the eighth and final contest. "It's not something I'm really proud of," Clarke recently noted, "but I honestly can't say I was ashamed to do it."

"Clarke is our leader," noted Flyers goalie

Bernie Parent. "He works so hard himself that the other guys just have to work to keep up. He is the guy who makes us go." Clarke was indeed visibly industrious, with his head bobbing as he raced around the ice, but he was also a gifted player. He danced with the puck and threaded slick passes to his teammates. Yet there were games when Clarke did seem to dig deeper than humanly possible, dragging his team up by the bootstraps to victory, particularly in the 1974 Stanley Cup final.

Facing the powerful Boston Bruins, Clarke's Flyers were down 2–0 in Game 2 after losing the series opener. Clarke scored once to narrow Boston's lead, and then he tied the game with only 52 seconds left in regulation time. With 12 minutes gone in overtime, Clarke concluded a magnificent evening's work by completing a hat trick. The Bruins never fully recovered, and Clarke delivered the coup de grâce in the deciding game when he lured Bobby Orr into hauling him down with just over two minutes remaining. With Orr sitting in the penalty box, the Flyers won the game 1–0 and hoisted the Stanley Cup for the first time.

Clarke served two terms as Philadelphia's general manager, using the same approach with his club that he used so successfully as a player and consistently constructing big and tough Stanley Cup contenders. He currently serves as a club vice-president.

AWARDS: 1st All-Star (2), 2nd All-Star (2), Hart (3), Masterton, Pearson, Selke, Stanley Cup (2), HHOF 1987

STATS:

	GP	G	A	Pts	PIM
RS	1,144	358	852	1,210	1,453
PO	136	42	77	119	152

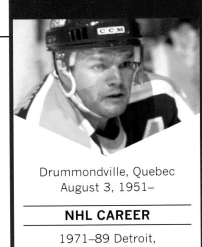

Drummondville, Quebec
August 3, 1951–

NHL CAREER

1971–89 Detroit,
Los Angeles, NY Rangers

MARCEL DIONNE

On skates, he was as solid as a fire hydrant and not much bigger, but Marcel Dionne had quick acceleration and an aggressive run-and-gun style that put him in the spotlight at a young age. Family and hometown pressures in Quebec were so great during his teenage years that the scoring sensation opted to play in Ontario's junior league, where, in spite of the culture shock he experienced, he won two consecutive scoring championships.

Dionne stood just under 5-foot-8, but NHL scouts ranked him with Guy Lafleur, his perennial rival in Quebec. After some dithering, the Montreal Canadiens selected Lafleur as the number-one pick in the 1971 NHL entry draft, and the Detroit Red Wings quickly snapped up Dionne with the second pick.

Dionne had an auspicious rookie year, with 28 goals and 49 assists, but his team was in turmoil. Problems at the top of the Red Wings organization trickled down to the players.

Dionne was suspended from the team twice for arguing with his coach. "You have to find a way to survive," maintained Dionne. He racked up 366 points in four seasons with the Red Wings and moved into the top tier of the league's scoring race, finishing behind Bobby Orr and Phil Esposito in the 1974–75 season. However, Dionne and the Red Wings never got a hint of playoff action together.

Discouraged by the losing atmosphere in the Motor City, Dionne became the first high-profile player to test the new free-agent market. In 1975 the Los Angeles Kings made a generous offer, and Dionne jumped at the chance to play for a team that had been rising consistently in the standings. Unfortunately, Dionne soon found himself in a familiar situation. While the Kings enjoyed little success during the almost 12 seasons he spent in Los Angeles, Dionne remained an offensive force. In his second season in LA's purple and gold, he broke the 50-goal plateau for the first of six times in seven years.

His clean play twice earned him the Lady Byng Trophy; he also won the Art Ross Trophy, but by the narrowest of margins. Dionne had to come up with two assists in the final game of the 1979–80 campaign to match Gretzky's late-

AWARDS: 1st All-Star (2), 2nd All-Star (2), Byng (2), Pearson (2), Ross, HHOF 1992

STATS:

	GP	G	A	Pts	PIM
RS	1,348	731	1,040	1,771	600
PO	49	21	24	45	17

season surge to 137 points. Dionne got the title, with 53 goals versus Gretzky's 51.

Dionne appreciated his trophies, but he valued none so much as the Pearson Award for the league's MVP (as voted by the players), which he won in 1979 and again in 1980. Dionne had lost respect for the hockey writers when they had voted him center for the First All-Star Team for the 1976–77 season. "I played the right wing in the Canada Cup that September," he explained. "I went back to Los Angeles, played the whole year at right wing, and they voted for me at center." His success that season notwithstanding, Dionne was soon back in the pivot position, where his freewheeling style gave defensemen nightmares. Dave Taylor and Charlie Simmer joined him at his flanks, and the "Triple Crown Line" quickly gathered notice as one of the NHL's best.

Ostensibly for a shot at a Stanley Cup, Dionne demanded a trade in 1986–87, although he later claimed that his request was a contract-negotiation ploy. To his dismay, he became a New York Ranger. "My heart is still with the Kings," the outspoken star admitted with controversial candor two weeks later, "but my body is with the Rangers."

Dionne moved into third place in career goals scored, but as his always-churning

legs started to slow, the goals came further and further apart. "Because you love the game so much," said Dionne, "you think it will never end." He spent nine games in the minors before retiring in 1989.

Sault Ste. Marie, Ontario
February 20, 1942–

NHL CAREER

1963–81 Chicago, Boston,
NY Rangers

PHIL ESPOSITO

Phil Esposito was blessed with many skills as a hockey player, but it was his passion that set him apart. He shattered the single-season scoring record, won five scoring championships and helped lead his team to two Stanley Cup victories. Yet his emotional nature had its greatest impact at the midpoint of the historic 1972 Summit Series.

The roundly favored Canadians had just suffered their second defeat to the Soviets, concluding their home half of the series with a win, a tie and two losses. An angry Vancouver crowd booed Team Canada. "We gave it our best," scolded an obviously exhausted Esposito in a televised interview. "All of us guys are really disheartened… We came out because we love Canada. And I don't think it is fair that we should be booed." Few watching were unmoved. The nation rallied behind the team, which eked out a slim and miraculous series victory. Paul Henderson's winning goals in the last three games are forever etched into the Canadian consciousness, but Esposito's leadership and effectiveness on the ice — he led the series in scoring — were arguably even more crucial.

If Esposito had a weakness it was his skating, but he was a hulking bear of a man who became an immovable object when he parked himself in front of the net. At the age of 19, he caught on with the St. Catharines Teepees, a junior team affiliated with the Chicago Black Hawks.

Esposito served a three-year apprenticeship in the minors, and when he finally earned a permanent spot in the NHL, for the 1964–65 season, it was a golden one. He centered a line with Bobby Hull on his left. With Esposito feeding him, Hull enjoyed seasons of 39, 54 and 52 goals. Esposito put the puck in the net too, although his detractors claimed many of them were "garbage" goals, a charge he faced throughout his career.

"Espo" was sent to the Boston Bruins in 1967 in one of the most lopsided trades in NHL history. He joined Ken Hodge and Fred Stanfield in Boston, while Pit Martin, Gilles Marotte and goalie Jack Norris went to Chicago. Hodge and Stanfield became key elements in a powerhouse Boston club, and Esposito achieved even greater heights.

AWARDS: 1st All-Star (6), 2nd All-Star (2), Hart (2), Pearson (2), Ross (5), Stanley Cup (2), HHOF 1984

STATS:

	GP	G	A	Pts	PIM
RS	1,282	717	873	1,590	910
PO	130	61	76	137	138

He won the Art Ross Trophy in his second season in Beantown, after finishing second to Chicago's Stan Mikita the previous year. He earned runner-up status again in 1970 (to teammate Bobby Orr), but he erupted the next season with a 76-goal, 76-assist campaign, eclipsing Bobby Hull's 58-goal record, which was set the previous year. In fact, Esposito had raised the bar so high that it would be 20 years before his single-season records started falling — to a young player named Wayne Gretzky.

Esposito dominated the dressing room, as well as the scoring race, with his gregarious manner and a penchant for superstition. His locker was festooned with good-luck charms, and he made sure that no one left hockey sticks crossed on the floor, for fear they would create bad luck.

Esposito and Orr were the linchpins of the Bruins' success and two Stanley Cup victories, but when the team began to falter in 1975, Boston's general manager, Harry Sinden, felt that a shake-up was needed. Esposito and Carol Vadnais went to their archrival, the New York Rangers, in return for Brad Park, Jean Ratelle and Joe Zanussi. While he never challenged for the scoring title again, Esposito won legions of fans in the Big Apple and took the Rangers to the Stanley Cup final in 1979. He retired in 1981, second only to Gordie Howe in NHL career goals and points scored.

WAYNE GRETZKY

Brantford, Ontario
January 26, 1961–

NHL CAREER

1978–99 Edmonton,
Los Angeles, St. Louis,
NY Rangers

Although everyone knew Wayne Gretzky's career would eventually end, it was a sad day for hockey when he announced his retirement at the end of the 1998–99 season. Gretzky, already the owner of 61 NHL records, including almost all of the most significant scoring records, decided to hang up his skates before he slipped out of the NHL elite. Ovations and accolades followed Gretzky's final game in Madison Square Garden, and the NHL announced the most fitting tribute of all: No player on any team will ever wear Gretzky's No. 99 again.

Like Abe Lincoln's log cabin in America, the Gretzky backyard rink is a part of Canadian folklore. Even as a child, Gretzky was the center of national attention: At age 10, he scored 378 goals in a 69-game season, and in 1978, at age 17, he signed his first professional contract, with the Indianapolis Racers of the WHA. Gretzky's contract was soon sold to Peter Pocklington, owner of the Edmonton Oilers.

"The pace seems a little faster in this league," he commented when his team joined the NHL, "but the WHA was a good league. I feel I did well for my first year. I will do my best and hope it's good enough." A "merger" rule disqualified Gretzky from Calder Trophy voting, and he suffered further disappointment when his 51 goals and 86 assists left him tied with Marcel Dionne for total points. Dionne was awarded the scoring crown based on his 53 goals. "I was always taught that an assist is as good as a goal," stated Gretzky tersely, but for the next seven years he beat his closest rival by an average of 66 points.

"Wayne kind of sneaks up on you," Edmonton coach Glen Sather once remarked. "He doesn't have Bobby Hull's power or Bobby Orr's speed, but he has the same magic."

Orr himself was amazed. "You figure a guy has Gretzky trapped. Next thing you know, Gretzky has given the puck to somebody you figure he couldn't even see."

While admitting to often "sensing" where his teammates are, Gretzky believes his celebrated vision was honed by fear. He had always played against older, bigger and stronger opponents. "I couldn't beat people with my strength," the slight superstar once explained. "My eyes and my mind have to do most of the work."

While his natural gifts were awesome, Gretzky had always been a hard worker. "First, you have to have a passion and a love for the sport," he declared. "Second, you have to have a dedication to it."

He dominated the NHL during the regular season — most notably with his 92 goals and

120 assists in the 1981–82 campaign and his 52 goals and 163 assists in 1985–86 — but Gretzky also enjoyed post-season success. "Kids grow up dreaming about holding up the Stanley Cup," he once said. "That dream fuels you in the playoffs." But after leading Edmonton to four Stanley Cups, "The Great One" was essentially sold to the Los Angeles Kings in 1988.

His "trade" was seen by many Canadians as a national disaster, but his presence invigorated the LA franchise and stimulated NHL growth throughout the southern United States. Gretzky won three more scoring championships in Los Angeles, but he requested a trade to a contender in 1995–96. After a short stay in St. Louis, he headed for Broadway and the New York Rangers. After three seasons in Manhattan, Gretzky bade his tearful goodbye.

Post-retirement, Gretzky became part owner of the Phoenix Coyotes. He successfully served as general manager of Team Canada, which won a 2002 Olympic gold medal and the 2004 World Cup. After the NHL lockout of 2004–05, he stepped behind the Coyotes' bench. Over four seasons, Gretzky's results were uneven, but the team's financial state and the uncertainty over whether the franchise would move led Gretzky to resign before the coaching phase of his career was fully tested. Although he now makes his home in California, Wayne Gretzky remains one of Canada's favorite sons.

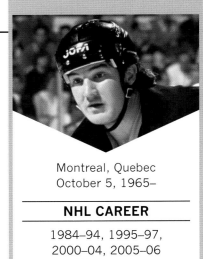

Montreal, Quebec
October 5, 1965–

NHL CAREER

1984–94, 1995–97,
2000–04, 2005–06
Pittsburgh

MARIO LEMIEUX

Mario Lemieux scored on the first shift of his first NHL game with his first shot on net. No other player has ever made so auspicious a debut. The Pittsburgh Penguins selected Lemieux with the first pick in the 1984 NHL entry draft, refusing tempting offers for proven NHL players. The highly touted junior — he scored 282 points in his last season — stepped right into the NHL and won the Calder Trophy with his first 100-point season, notching 43 goals. Disbelievers accused Lemieux of neglecting his defensive responsibilities, but the Penguins were looking for offense and Lemieux delivered.

The 1985 NHL All-Star Game offered Lemieux the perfect stage to silence his critics. He scored twice and had one helper in leading his team to victory. He was named the game's MVP, an honor he would receive twice more in the next five years, yet the Penguins continued to languish near the league's cellar.

Lemieux played brilliantly for Canada in the 1987 Canada Cup tournament, and with 168 points he dethroned Gretzky as league scoring champion in the 1987–88 season. He retained the title with an amazing 199 points the following year. When the Penguins made the playoffs that year, Lemieux had fulfilled one of his primary goals.

The team slipped in 1989–90, however, and failed to qualify for post-season action (Lemieux missed 21 games because of a herniated disk in his back, but he still managed to amass 123 points), and Lemieux's detractors were vocal once more.

After Lemieux's back surgery that summer, a deep infection set in, and the center missed the first 50 games of the regular season. But he came back, tallied 45 points in 26 games and almost matched that total with 16 goals and 44 points in the playoffs. After raising the Stanley Cup in victory, he was awarded the Conn Smythe Trophy.

Lemieux punctuated that glorious achievement in the 1991–92 season with another scoring title, his second Conn Smythe Trophy and a Stanley Cup ring. He will be best remembered, however, for his heroics the following year.

Lemieux was diagnosed with Hodgkin's disease and underwent two months of grueling radiation

AWARDS: 1st All-Star (6), 2nd All-Star (4), Calder, Hart (3), Masterton, Pearson (4), Ross (6), Smythe (2), Stanley Cup (2), HHOF 1997

STATS:

	GP	G	A	Pts	PIM
RS	915	690	1,033	1,723	834
PO	107	76	96	172	87

treatment before rejoining the Penguins. He went on to win his fourth Art Ross Trophy by a 12-point margin. The Penguins finished atop the league, and although they failed to win the Cup again, Lemieux won his second Hart Trophy (MVP), his third Pearson Award (players' choice for MVP) and the Bill Masterton Trophy (for his perseverance and dedication to the game).

The next season, Lemieux missed 58 games due to complications from further back surgery. Still anemic from the radiation therapy, an exhausted Lemieux sat out the entire 1994–95 season to recuperate. But he made a reassuring pronouncement: "I'm not coming back to be an average player." He proved his point by winning the scoring championship the next two seasons.

Still, Lemieux was not happy. He began to talk of retirement, citing both a desire to spend more time with his young family and a distaste for the game of clutching, hooking and grabbing that the NHL tolerated.

True to his word, the 31-year-old hung up his skates at the end of the 1996–97 season. The Hockey Hall of Fame inducted Lemieux immediately, but his playing days weren't over. When the Penguins were at risk of going bankrupt, Lemieux brokered a deal to keep the team afloat by taking an ownership position and

returning to play in 2000–01. "Super Mario" showed why he will always be remembered as one of the game's most illustrious stars — he even captained Team Canada to win an Olympic gold medal in 2002 — before retiring for good in 2005. As an owner, he has mentored Sidney Crosby — even playing alongside him for a few months in 2005–06 — and Lemieux joined his players on the ice to hoist another Stanley Cup in 2009.

MARK MESSIER

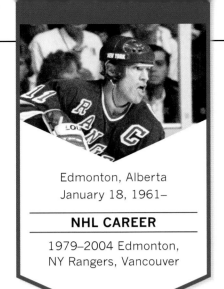

Edmonton, Alberta
January 18, 1961–

NHL CAREER

1979–2004 Edmonton,
NY Rangers, Vancouver

"I can never shrug off a defeat," Mark Messier has said. "I can remember a friend of mine — a rookie and a real competitor — on a team that hadn't done well for years. He'd be upset after a loss, and the veterans would say, 'Listen, don't worry about it. There's nothing you can do.' That's why some teams never get turned around. They accept losing." Only Messier has captained two different teams to the Stanley Cup.

Messier was 17 years old when he turned professional with the Indianapolis Racers in 1979. Ironically, he was brought in to replace Wayne Gretzky, who had been sold to Edmonton. Although he scored only one goal that year, Messier was drafted by the Edmonton Oilers when the NHL swallowed the rival league that summer.

Mean, with a fierce glare, "Moose" learned to use his speed and aggression to record his first and only 50-goal season in 1981–82, at the same time making the First All-Star Team. He broke the 100-point barrier the following season and had 15 playoff goals before being injured prior to the final round. Post-season success, however, was his destiny.

Messier was at his best when the young Oilers faced the veteran New York Islanders in the 1984 Stanley Cup final. In the third game of the series,

he scored a dramatic goal, and the Islanders didn't recover. Messier won the Conn Smythe Trophy winner as playoff MVP. He continued to earn All-Star status and was a huge part of Edmonton's first four Stanley Cups, always scoring at least 25 playoff points. However, it took a separation from Gretzky to bring Messier to his highest heights.

Messier became Edmonton's captain in 1988, when Gretzky was essentially sold to the Los Angeles Kings. He hit a career high with 129 points in 1989–90 and won both the Hart Trophy and the Pearson Award. Messier then led all playoff scorers by contributing 22 assists toward Edmonton's fifth Stanley Cup win. "I don't think we could have pulled it off without Mark," said teammate Craig Simpson. "He held us all together."

Continuing to sell off its assets, Edmonton sent Messier to the Rangers just before the 1991–92 season got under way. He stormed Manhattan and earned the Hart Trophy and the Pearson Award again. "The players talk about what it would be like to skate around Madison Square Garden with the Cup," said Messier, not one to rest on his laurels. "And we talk about what it would be like to have a parade down Broadway. You've got to visualize these things if you want to make them happen." After a disappointing

1992–93 season, Messier took a great risk in the 1993–94 playoffs. Down 3–2 to the New Jersey Devils after five games in the Eastern Conference final, Messier offered a guarantee. "We know we are going to go in there and win Game 6 and bring it back to the Garden," he announced. The Rangers had their backs tightly against the wall, trailing 2–1 after two periods, before Messier took over and notched a third-period hat trick to secure the game. The Rangers prevailed in Game 7 and against Vancouver in the Cup final, and Messier had his sixth Cup ring.

"There aren't any motives for me other than wanting to compete and win," said free-agent Messier when he signed a three-year contract with Vancouver in 1997. "It begins and ends with that." Canuck fans were hopeful the man many regarded as the best leader in the history of the game would lead their team to the promised land, but it wasn't to be. After three disappointing seasons, Messier rejoined the Rangers. Although his team floundered, Messier remained a consistent performer until retiring in 2004. "When I hear that legend talk, I actually feel a little guilty, a little embarrassed," remarked Messier. "One player, no matter how good a leader on and off the ice, does not win the Stanley Cup. Your teammates have to have the same burning desire as you." Messier sits second all-time in regular season points, playoff points and regular season games.

AWARDS: 1st All-Star (4), 2nd All-Star, Hart (2), Pearson (2), Smythe, Stanley Cup (6), HHOF 2007

STATS:

	GP	G	A	Pts	PIM
RS	1,756	694	1,193	1,887	1,910
PO	236	109	186	295	244

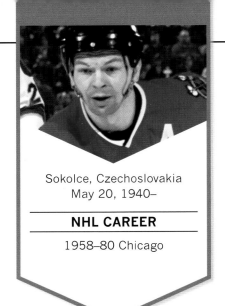

Sokolce, Czechoslovakia
May 20, 1940–

NHL CAREER

1958–80 Chicago

STAN MIKITA

Many of the meanest men on ice turn into the most kind people once they step off it, but Stan Mikita took that character transformation in a different direction. The once-chippy, frequently penalized scoring whiz drastically reduced his time in the penalty box while remaining the league's top playmaker. He was awarded the Lady Byng Trophy (most gentlemanly player), the Art Ross Trophy (most points) and the Hart Trophy (most valuable player) at the end of the 1966–67 and 1967–68 seasons. No one else has ever won that triumvirate of awards in one season, let alone two.

On May 20, 1940, Mikita was born Stanislav Guoth in Sokolce, Czechoslovakia. Reflecting on their poverty and uncertain future, his parents decided in 1948 that it would be in their son's best interest to join his aunt and uncle, who had immigrated to Canada. The Mikitas of St. Catharines, Ontario, adopted Stan as their

son, and he soon discovered hockey.

He excelled at the game, and hockey allowed him to avenge the taunts he faced because of his strongly accented English. "I wasn't going to be pushed around or laughed at," Mikita explained. "That egged me on, made me perform better. I said I was going to be better than those guys." Small but fiery, Mikita carried a chip on his shoulder for years.

That all changed when Mikita married and became a father. Asked by his young daughter why he had to sit by himself so often (in the penalty box), Mikita was embarrassed by his own answer. He determined to curb his anger and work harder while sacrificing nothing on the score sheet.

Mikita won only one Stanley Cup, in 1961, and he led all playoff scorers that season. His most productive years were still to come, though, and the "Scooter Line" (Mikita between Doug Mohns and Ken Wharram) gave opposition goalies trouble for five years in the 1960s. Red Kelly, who faced Mikita on defense, at center and behind the bench, paid tribute when he stated, "Mikita would fool you, because he could always pull something extra out of the hat. He was tricky, a good stickhandler and one of the best faceoff men in the business."

AWARDS: 1st All-Star (6), 2nd All-Star (2), Byng (2), Hart (2), Ross (4), Stanley Cup, HHOF 1983

STATS:

	GP	G	A	Pts	PIM
RS	1,394	541	926	1,467	1,270
PO	155	59	91	150	169

Mikita's constant tinkering led to his accidental discovery of the benefits of the curved stick in 1961. He noticed how the puck behaved unpredictably when he fired a shot in frustration with a stick blade cracked into a severe hook. After further experimentation, the "banana blade" was born — and eventually banned. Mikita was also one of the first players to wear a helmet as a preventive measure. Soon, his own improved helmet design was on the market.

Despite Mikita's many achievements, he remained in the shadow of his teammate Bobby Hull for most of his long career. Mikita and Hull first played together in high school, then in junior hockey and finally with the Black Hawks. Hull's explosive power and beaming smile contrasted sharply with Mikita's sometimes abrasive personality, acerbic wit and use of finesse over brawn. Mikita, who always denied resenting Hull, once explained, "I played hard and got the job done. But I didn't lift fans out of their seats doing it, and Bobby did."

Still, when he scored his 500th career goal in Chicago Stadium on February 27, 1977, the crowd's roar was ear-splitting. Mikita's No. 21 was officially retired by the Black Hawks the season after he hung up his skates — he was the first player to be so honored in that franchise's history. And fittingly, Hull and Mikita entered the Hockey Hall of Fame together in 1983.

HOWIE MORENZ

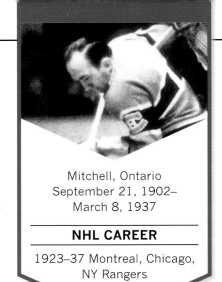

Mitchell, Ontario
September 21, 1902–
March 8, 1937

NHL CAREER

1923–37 Montreal, Chicago,
NY Rangers

It was a funeral unlike any seen before in Canada. On March 11, 1937, Howie Morenz's body lay in state at center ice in the Montreal Forum. In three hours, more than 50,000 mourners filed past Morenz's casket. An estimated 250,000 people lined the route of his funeral procession. Hockey had lost one of its greatest stars.

Morenz earned the nickname "Mitchell Meteor" with his hometown Mitchell Juveniles. Morenz's next team, in nearby Stratford, won a provincial title in 1921, and the "Stratford Streak" caught the attention of the Montreal Canadiens.

After reluctantly agreeing to play for Montreal two years later, a homesick Morenz tried to break his contract and headed back to Mitchell during his first training camp. Cecil Hart of the Canadiens went after him, and when he placed $850 cash — Morenz's signing bonus — on the kitchen table, he convinced the whole Morenz family that Howie should return to Montreal.

Morenz quickly became famous for his blazing rushes and reckless style of hockey. Seemingly able to accelerate to top speed in a single stride, he helped establish Montreal's growing reputation for "firewagon" hockey. By the end of his rookie NHL year, in 1923–24, Morenz was tied for eighth in league scoring and had helped Montreal win its first Stanley Cup since 1916. Morenz eventually

won two scoring crowns and was named the league's most valuable player three times.

"He could adjust to any situation," recalled King Clancy in 1964. "He could barge between a defense, or he could poke a puck between your legs, then wheel around you and pick it up. His shot was just like a bullet, and he didn't fool around looking for an opening, he just let it go."

In a game against the New York Rangers during his second NHL season, Morenz knocked out four of Bun Cook's front teeth with the butt end of his stick while digging for the puck. Morenz immediately dropped his stick and helped Cook off the ice. "It was just an accident," explained Cook after the game. "Howie wouldn't pull anything like that intentionally."

Cook's feelings were later echoed by Boston's notorious Eddie Shore. "Everybody likes Howie," said Shore. "He's the one player who doesn't deserve any rough treatment."

Yet years of success and admiration didn't stop the Canadiens from trading Morenz to the Chicago Black Hawks in the summer of 1934. He had started to slow down the previous season. Leo Dandurand, general manager of the Canadiens, lent a little dignity to the situation when he retired Morenz's No. 7. Morenz sadly accepted his fate, but he hated Chicago. Halfway through his second mediocre season with the Black Hawks he was traded again, this time to the New York Rangers. He finished out the 1935–36 season as a Ranger, but when his old admirer Cecil Hart was installed as Montreal's new general manager that summer, Morenz became a Hab again.

His return to Montreal seemed to be a tonic for Morenz, and he began to show signs of his old magic. Then tragedy struck. In a game on January 7, 1937, Morenz was knocked down and slid into the boards. His skate jammed into the boards, and his leg snapped. Five fractures above the ankle forced him to spend weeks convalescing in hospital.

On March 8, at the age of 34, he died in his sleep of a coronary embolism. More than 60 years later, Howie Morenz Jr. disclosed a nurse's long-held confession — a doctor had postponed treating blood clots that had been detected in his leg the night of his death until morning. A romantic legend was debunked: "When he realized that he would never play again, he couldn't live with it," Morenz's teammate Aurèle Joliat had claimed. "I think Howie died of a broken heart."

AWARDS: 1st All-Star (2), 2nd All-Star, Hart (3), Stanley Cup (3), HHOF 1945

STATS:

	GP	G	A	Pts	PIM
RS	550	271	201	472	546
PO	39	13	9	22	58

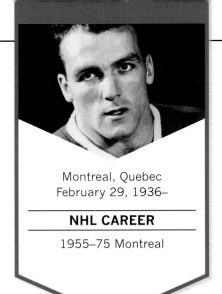

Montreal, Quebec
February 29, 1936–

NHL CAREER

1955–75 Montreal

HENRI RICHARD

"I was just mad. I didn't really mean it," claimed Henri Richard, although he had gone on record proclaiming that Al MacNeil was the worst coach he'd ever played for. In his first term at the helm, MacNeil had benched Richard for the fifth game of the 1971 Stanley Cup final, which had made the veteran center livid.

Richard went on to tie the deciding seventh game then potted the winner to defeat the Chicago Black Hawks 3–2 and thereby earn his 10th Stanley Cup ring. "I could have been a bum," Richard admitted, as the Canadiens were one game away from defeat, "and instead, I was a hero." He was also gracious enough to admit that MacNeil might have successfully inspired him to greater feats, but MacNeil resigned his position anyway.

Although he was never as dynamic as his older brother, Maurice, known to most simply as "The Rocket," Henri Richard made his own mark on the game. Even after Henri's successful junior

career, many thought the Canadiens were merely placating his brother when they signed him, as he never grew bigger than 5-foot-7 and 160 pounds. "He's a little small yet," Montreal coach Toe Blake said in 1955, when Henri joined the Canadiens, "but with his speed, we keep telling him not to try to go through the big opposition defensemen, just go around them."

"Once you are alone with a goaler," Richard eventually answered his critics, "size doesn't matter." But the shy, soft-spoken rookie let his first season's 19 goals do most of his talking. "Sometimes I think my size was an advantage," he noted, after heeding Blake's advice, "especially when I developed a crouching style. A big defenseman was often at a disadvantage. He'd even tumble over me if he tried to use his body rather than his stick."

Centering a line with Maurice on his right, at the Rocket's request, and Dickie Moore on left wing, Henri Richard made a major contribution to the five consecutive Stanley Cup victories he enjoyed in his first five NHL campaigns. He led the league in assists in 1957–58, earning a spot on the First All-Star Team.

Moore won two scoring championships, and many felt "The Pocket Rocket's" presence made Maurice a more complete player. From Maurice's

AWARDS: 1st All-Star, 2nd All-Star (3), Masterton, Stanley Cup (11), HHOF 1979

STATS:

	GP	G	A	Pts	PIM
RS	1,256	358	688	1,046	928
PO	180	49	80	129	181

point of view, his brother extended his career by a year or two: Henri worked so hard, he made Maurice's job easier. In the spring of 1960, Maurice retired. Although Henri was never the goal-scorer Maurice had been — and few were — he eventually set the family records for assists, points and seasons.

Blake was one of Richard's biggest boosters. "He's smart enough to be where the puck is all the time," Blake said in 1957. "He sizes up how a play is going to go, and then he gets there. And sometimes when he doesn't have things figured out in advance, he's so fast that he gets there first anyway."

Richard played doggedly, immune to intimidation — never betraying fear despite scrapping with some of the biggest and most aggressive players in the NHL. Moore expressed a sentiment shared by many: "Henri Richard might have been the toughest competitor I played with."

As goalie Gump Worsley noted, "Henri would get bounced around and always come back for more, stronger and faster than ever."

When Jean Beliveau retired in 1971, Henri Richard assumed the team captaincy and hoisted the Stanley Cup for the last time two seasons later. Silver-haired by then, he continued for two more years and entered his 20th NHL campaign. But after a broken ankle was slow to heal, he decided that he'd "better quit before it's too late." Montreal won the Cup for four consecutive years after he retired, but Henri Richard had no regrets. His 11 Stanley Cup rings stand as a record that will likely never be broken.

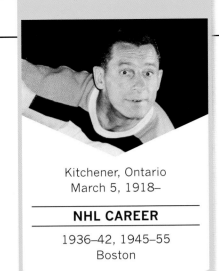

Kitchener, Ontario
March 5, 1918–

NHL CAREER

1936–42, 1945–55
Boston

MILT SCHMIDT

The Bruins' "Kraut Line" — hard-nosed center Milt Schmidt between elegant right winger Bobby Bauer and the tenacious Woody Dumart on the left side — was at the height of its power when World War II interrupted the trio's NHL careers. "It was our last game before we went into service," said Schmidt, recalling February 10, 1942, "and we had a fine night against the Canadiens at the Garden. I think we racked up 10 or 11 scoring points, and when the game was over, the other players on both teams picked us up on their shoulders and skated us off the ice while the crowd gave us an ovation." Although Schmidt was a member of two Stanley Cup–championship teams and won the Hart Trophy in 1951, that evening in 1942 remained a personal highlight. "A man could never forget a thing like that," he fondly reminisced.

Originally known as the "Sauerkraut Line," all three Kitchener-born players shared a German heritage and an uncommon bond. "We clicked first as personalities," said Schmidt, "then as hockey players." It was Dumart and Bauer who convinced the Boston Bruins to give their young friend Schmidt a shot at an NHL career. Their loyalty was rewarded when their line became the NHL's first to finish 1–2–3 in the scoring race. Schmidt was the NHL's leading scorer, with 52 points over the 48-game 1939–40 season, and Dumart and Bauer followed with 43 points apiece.

All three returned to the NHL from the armed services, with Schmidt hitting his personal high of 62 points in the 1946–47 season, but Bauer retired at the end of that season. Schmidt and Dumart were honored together with a "Schmidt/Dumart Night" on March 18, 1952. The fans had a treat in store: Bauer suited up for the evening and scored a goal on a pass from Schmidt, and both Bauer and Dumart assisted on Schmidt's 200th NHL goal.

"[Schmidt] was tough," recalled Montreal defenseman Butch Bouchard, "a big guy, and he was one of the best skaters I ever saw. He gave me a big shift one night in my first year. When I went to the bench, Dick Irvin [Montreal's coach] asked me if I had caught a cold because of the breeze that Schmidt made when he went by me." Schmidt also served as the team "policeman"

AWARDS: 1st All-Star (3), 2nd All-Star, Hart, Stanley Cup (2), HHOF 1961

STATS:

	GP	G	A	Pts	PIM
RS	776	229	346	575	466
PO	86	24	25	49	60

and waged a personal war with Detroit's "Black" Jack Stewart, one of the meanest defensemen in the NHL.

"Oh, we had some dandies," Schmidt laughed years later, "but we both finally wised up. We still had to earn a living!"

"I never backed away from anyone. I never let up while I was on the ice," Schmidt recalled at the end of his playing career, when he moved immediately into coaching. "I expect my players to be that way too."

"Milt will be a good coach," said Schmidt's former teammate Lynn Patrick, who stepped into the position of general manager when Schmidt replaced him as coach during the 1954–55 season, "but he'll lack one thing that has made me successful. When things get really tough for him, he won't be able to get out of the jam just by

looking down the bench and yelling, 'Okay, Milt, get out there.'"

It was as Boston's general manager, however, that Schmidt achieved his greatest success off the ice. In 1967 he engineered the deal that brought Phil Esposito, Ken Hodge and Fred Stanfield to Boston from Chicago, a turning point for the Bruins that led to Stanley Cup victories in 1970 and 1972.

When the Washington Capitals asked him to manage their inaugural squad in 1974, Schmidt took a brief hiatus from the Bruins organization. He fired two coaches and ensconced himself behind the bench, but his team lost 95 times in 116 games. Schmidt resigned just after Christmas in 1975. Fittingly, he eventually returned to work for the Bruins, who had retired his No. 15 in 1955.

NELS STEWART

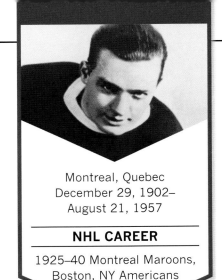

Montreal, Quebec
December 29, 1902–
August 21, 1957

NHL CAREER

1925–40 Montreal Maroons,
Boston, NY Americans

Nels Stewart was known as "Old Poison" for the quick and deadly way he put the puck in the net. On January 3, 1931, he set a record that still stands, scoring two goals four seconds apart, but by then Stewart had already established his reputation. After spending five seasons with Cleveland in the old U.S. Amateur Hockey Association, Stewart burst into the NHL with the Montreal Maroons in 1925–26. His 34 goals in the 36-game campaign led the league, as did his 42 scoring points. The Maroons won the Stanley Cup, Stewart scoring the winning goal in each of his team's victories over the Victoria Cougars in a best-of-five series.

"In some ways, 1925 was the high spot in my career, which had only started," recalled Stewart. "I won the rookie award and the Hart Trophy. I showed I could take it and dish it out too." His 119 penalty minutes were only two fewer than league leader Bert Corbeau's, and the following year Stewart led with 133 minutes. After spending a couple of seasons on right wing, he moved to center in 1929 between ideal wingers. The "S-Line" became one of the league's most potent. "Hooley Smith and Babe Siebert did most of the work," Stewart said humbly. "They knew I was out there waiting, and if they freed the puck, I'd do the rest." Using his 200 pounds and 6-foot-1

frame to advantage in battling for position, Stewart also had a deft scoring touch.

"Goalmouth scrambles were my forte," he maintained. "I scored three-quarters of my goals by drifting in front of the goalmouth until the proper moment occurred. There's a trick in this, and I used every trick in the book." Stewart's stick had about half the average angle between shaft and blade. "I always used a lie-12, which stood almost straight up and down," he explained, "so I could control the puck close to my skates."

Back-checking was an activity Stewart pretty much left to others. "I was a lazy daisy who hung around the goal waiting for passes," he said, but economy of movement was critical when a player was on the ice for 45 to 50 minutes of every game. "I always figured someone else could stymie the opposition," he admitted. "My job was to score goals." A slow-moving skater, he used short, choppy strides — until he got the puck.

AWARDS: Hart (2), Stanley Cup, HHOF 1952

STATS:

	GP	G	A	Pts	PIM
RS	650	324	191	515	953
PO	50	9	12	21	47

In 1929–30, Stewart hit his career high of 39 goals and 55 points and earned a second Hart Trophy. His consistent scoring and aggressive play weren't enough to help the Maroons to a Stanley Cup victory, however, and he was traded to the Boston Bruins in 1932. He placed in the top 10 among NHL scoring leaders for three consecutive seasons before the New York Americans acquired him in 1935.

Stewart tied for the NHL lead with 23 tallies in the 1936–37 season, a noteworthy campaign that not only saw him traded back to Boston and returned to the Americans after just 10 games, but also saw him pass Howie Morenz to become the league's career leader in goals scored. Stewart held that distinction for 16 years. He became the first NHL player to score 300 goals, but the end was in sight. "My reflexes were slower," he said. "I lacked that extra step, and I hit the post instead of the net."

Stewart retired after the 1938–39 season, having eclipsed Morenz's career points record, but the Americans persuaded him to come back for one more year the next autumn. After seven more goals, seven assists and an almost saintly six penalty minutes in 35 games, "Old Poison" retired for good in 1940.

"Congratulations on breaking the record," read the telegram Stewart sent in 1952, the day after Maurice Richard broke his NHL career goal record of 324. "Hope it will hold for many seasons." Stewart did, however, remain the highest-scoring NHL centerman for 30 years,

until another Montreal Canadien, Jean Beliveau, bettered that mark in 1964.

Stewart was a regular visitor to Maple Leaf Gardens for years. "When I see that loose puck in front of the cage," he said in 1953, "my heart still jumps. That was the moment I always waited for." Sadly, Stewart died suddenly in 1957, at the age of 55. He was elected to the Hockey Hall of Fame five years later.

BRYAN TROTTIER

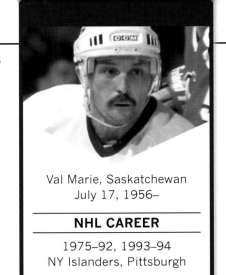

Val Marie, Saskatchewan
July 17, 1956–

NHL CAREER

1975–92, 1993–94
NY Islanders, Pittsburgh

Bryan Trottier has had as intimate a relationship with the Stanley Cup as any player — and then some. His six Stanley Cup rings bear testimony to his triumphs.

Trottier was selected by the Islanders in the 1974 entry draft as an underage player. He played a final year of junior hockey and got a lucrative offer from the Cincinnati Stingers of the WHA, but Trottier had eyes only for the NHL. As he told writer Roy MacGregor during his rookie season with the Islanders, "The dream has not come true. I am living the dream. And that's better." Trottier tallied 98 points and won Rookie of the Year honors. He was also seriously considered for the Lady Byng Trophy.

While only 5-foot-10, Trottier displayed a tenacity and single-mindedness that more than compensated for his size, and as his penalty minutes grew, a nastier side emerged. "Trottier's hidden talent," said Pittsburgh coach Johnny Wilson, "is that he looks like an altar boy and hits like a monster."

When the Islanders drafted sharpshooter Mike Bossy in 1977, Trottier received the perfect winger. In 1977–78, he led the league in assists, with 77, and finished second in points behind Guy Lafleur, earning a First All-Star Team selection. Trottier followed up with an even

more sensational year, adding the Art Ross and Hart Trophies to his list of accomplishments. Meanwhile, his team led the league during the 1978–79 regular season and was in the final stages of becoming a Stanley Cup threat.

The next season, Trottier led all playoff scorers, with 12 goals and 29 points, and was awarded the Conn Smythe Trophy as the Islanders won their first of four consecutive Stanley Cups. He notched his first and only 50-goal campaign in the 1980–81 season and led the playoffs in scoring again that spring, eclipsing Bobby Orr's playoff assist record by notching 23.

But that proved to be the last time Trottier would win a scoring race. After winning their third and fourth Stanley Cups in four-game sweeps, Trottier and the Islanders slipped back into the pack during the 1983–84 regular season. They clawed their way to the Stanley Cup final for the fifth consecutive time, but Wayne Gretzky

AWARDS: 1st All-Star (2), 2nd All-Star (2), Calder, Clancy, Hart, Ross, Smythe, Stanley Cup (6), HHOF 1997

STATS:

	GP	G	A	Pts	PIM
RS	1,279	524	901	1,425	912
PO	221	71	113	184	277

and his Edmonton Oilers finally dethroned the Islanders.

Trottier had played for Canada in the 1981 Canada Cup tournament, but in 1984 he decided to compete for the United States — invoking his Indian Status, which, in effect, gave him dual citizenship. "I want to give something back," he claimed, noting the United States allowed him to make a good living.

Trottier continued to rack up respectable point totals over the years, but his gritty play also helped him establish himself as one of the game's premier checkers. "I'm vocal when I think my opinion will accomplish something advantageous," he said in respect to his leadership role, and he enjoyed his place in the game.

On February 13, 1990, Trottier scored his 500th career goal, but he was stunned later that spring when the Islanders bought out the last two years of his contract. The terms, unfavorable to Trottier, sent his off-ice business interests into a downward spiral. He fell into a clinical depression and financial ruin, but he rebounded fully after receiving therapy and declaring bankruptcy. Pittsburgh added him to its roster, and Trottier helped the Penguins to Stanley Cup victories in 1991 and 1992.

In 1986, Trottier described how he wanted to be remembered: "As a consistently hard worker who gave his all on every shift; as a guy who, if he missed a check, kept coming back and gave that second and third effort; as a guy who just didn't quit."

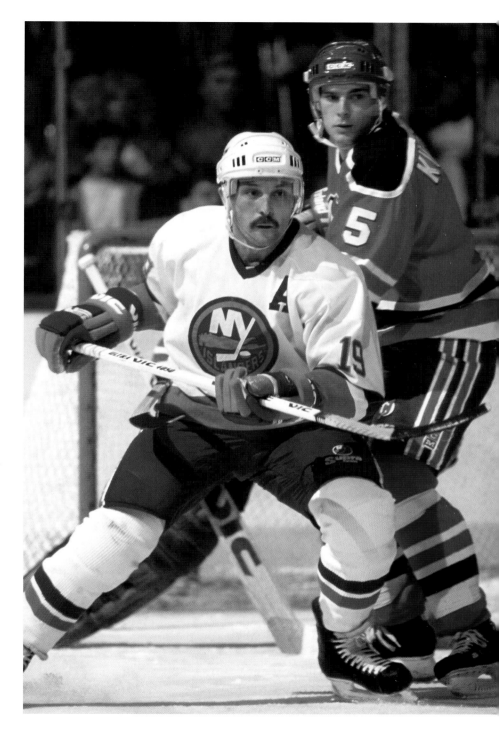

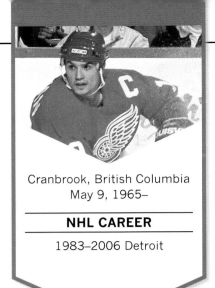

Cranbrook, British Columbia
May 9, 1965–

NHL CAREER

1983–2006 Detroit

STEVE YZERMAN

Having led the Detroit Red Wings to first-place finishes during the previous two regular seasons, Steve Yzerman had seen his team swept in the Stanley Cup final by New Jersey in 1995 and vanquished in the 1996 semifinals by the underdog Colorado Avalanche. That he lacked a championship ring was a knock against "Stevie Y" for years, but Yzerman remained undaunted. "My approach is to have fun," he said in the fall of 1996. "My desire to win the Cup hasn't changed at all, but I'm not consumed by it now. I want to experience the celebration of winning the Cup, of getting to carry it around the ice," he added. "I've dreamed about it since I was a kid."

Yzerman made his first mark on the game through his prodigious offensive skills. His 39 goals and 87 points as an 18-year-old rookie earned him an invitation to the 1984 All-Star Game. When he was made Red Wings captain in 1986, at the tender age of 21, Yzerman blossomed with the added responsibility.

Yzerman hit the magic 50-goal-season plateau in 1987–88 and topped 100 points for the first of six consecutive seasons. The following year, he peaked with 65 goals and 155 points. Only Wayne Gretzky and Mario Lemieux have ever posted higher numbers — which they did that year — but the NHL players voted "Stevie

Wonder" the league's outstanding player.

For close to a decade, Detroit's playoff shortcomings fueled constant speculation about whether Yzerman should be traded. "That's like asking me if I'd trade my son Jason for the kid next door," claimed Detroit's coach, Jacques Demers. Although Yzerman tallied 62 goals in the 1989–90 season, the Red Wings missed the playoffs, and it was Demers who got the pink slip. The Yzerman trade rumors ended soon after Scotty Bowman stepped behind the bench in 1993.

Yzerman was already a strong two-way player, but Bowman insisted that he change his approach somewhat. Taking his game up another level, Yzerman sacrificed the possibility of scoring championships while still remaining an offensive threat. His inspirational shot-blocking and ferocious back-checking set the tone, and within three years his team became the league's stingiest defensively, setting an NHL record with 62 regular-season victories. A quiet man in the dressing room, Yzerman spoke volumes with his actions, his eyes blazing with competitive fire.

Yzerman finally fulfilled his Stanley Cup dream in 1997; when the Red Wings took their second consecutive Stanley Cup in 1998, Yzerman was

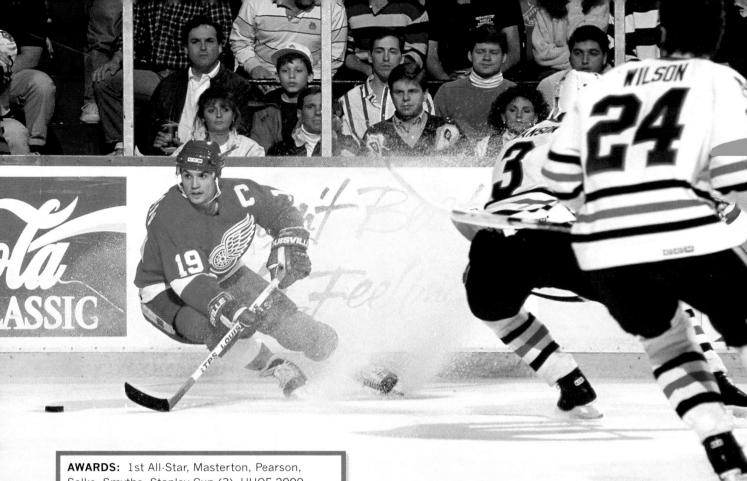

AWARDS: 1st All-Star, Masterton, Pearson, Selke, Smythe, Stanley Cup (3), HHOF 2009

STATS:

	GP	G	A	Pts	PIM
RS	1,514	692	1,063	1,755	924
PO	196	70	115	185	84

awarded the Conn Smythe Trophy. In 2002, hobbled by a knee injury suffered while winning an Olympic gold medal for Canada, he completed one of the grittiest performances in playoff history and hoisted the Cup for a third time.

Early in the 1998–99 season, Yzerman notched his 1,426th point, passing his boyhood hero Bryan Trottier and moving into 10th place on the NHL career points list. "Bryan Trottier was my favorite player," said Yzerman, who proudly wore Trottier's old No. 19 (officially retired by Detroit in 2007). "We all have role models, and he's mine. I followed his entire career as soon as he came into the league. In some ways, I tried to play like he did. In my mind, he is one of the best players ever."

"I had set a goal of 20 years that I'd like to play," he once said. "That is not necessarily set in stone, but I'd like to continue to play for as long as I feel I am an effective player and getting things done on the ice." Major knee surgery in summer 2002 cost Yzerman most of the following season, and an eye injury knocked him out of the 2004 playoffs. Yet he still felt he had gas left in the tank and played through the 2005–06 campaign, notching 14 goals and 20 assists in 61 games. He retired as the longest-serving captain of all time, not only in hockey but in all of North American major league sports.

Yzerman spent several years in Detroit's front office, and he was general manager of Team Canada for gold medal wins at the 2007 World Championship and the 2010 Olympics. In May of 2010, Yzerman became general manager of the Tampa Bay Lightning, where he continues to garner respect for his hockey acumen.

CENTERS

LIONS

Nicklas Backstrom 44
Sidney Crosby 46
Evgeni Malkin................................. 48
Steven Stamkos 50
Jonathan Toews............................... 52

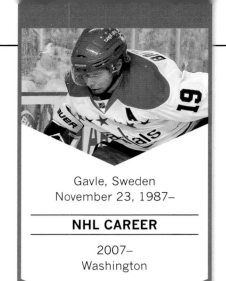

NICKLAS BACKSTROM

Gavle, Sweden
November 23, 1987–

NHL CAREER

2007–
Washington

Alex Ovechkin is the face of the Washington Capitals, and his linemate Nicklas Backstrom likes it that way. Unlike his extroverted winger, Backstrom is happy making the assists to the superstar, which he does with impressive frequency. "'Backs' is an unbelievable player," said Ovechkin. "If I play without him, maybe I don't get too many points; maybe I don't get too many goals."

Backstrom was a star for the Brynas IF club in his native Sweden, where he played his junior hockey and won the Elite League's Rookie of the Year award in 2005–06. As the youngest player to ever represent Sweden in a World Championship, in spring 2006 he went home with a gold medal and the thrill of playing on a line with his idols Henrik Zetterberg and Johan Franzen. More excitement ensued at the 2006 NHL draft. Ovechkin was given the honor of announcing Washington's first pick, fourth overall, and handed Backstrom his new Capitals sweater. But just as Backstrom displays outstanding patience with the puck and has a knack for being in the right place at the right time, he also had the maturity not to rush into the NHL.

After one more season in Sweden, Backstrom signed a three-year entry-level contract with the Capitals and made his NHL debut on October 5,

2007. He didn't miss a single game through three seasons, before finally being forced out of five contests late in 2010–11 with a thumb injury. Backstrom was initially the second-line center, but when the veteran Swede Michael Nylander went down with an injury, Backstrom was promoted to play with Ovechkin on the top line. After a brief period of adjustment, the two clicked, developing the kind of chemistry that terrifies the opposition. "I feel where he is," Ovechkin told the *Washington Post*. "He doesn't score lots of goals, but he's a great passer."

Ovechkin finished the 2007–08 season with an impressive 65 goals and the overall scoring championship with 112 points. As the runner-up for NHL Rookie of the Year honors, Backstrom tallied 14 goals and a team-leading 55 assists, finishing second overall in rookie scoring.

Although he's tough to knock off the puck — many compare Backstrom to Peter Forsberg because of his surprising ability to shield the puck, especially along the boards — and has carried defensemen on his back as he emerges from a scrum with the puck on his stick, Backstrom's real strength is his soft hands and deft touch. His slick flip pass has become a trademark, and he gets away with some risky-looking passes because they usually connect.

"I trust my brain," said Backstrom, commenting on his ability to spot openings. "It's my best thing on the ice, the way I see the ice."

In 2008–09, Backstrom played in his first NHL All-Star Game, and he finished tenth in league scoring (22) and fourth in assists (66). The following season, he jumped to fourth in total scoring, with 33 goals and 68 assists, helping the Capitals finish high atop the 2009–10 regular season standings. However, he has earned praise for more than just his offensive skills. Canadian broadcaster TSN co-awarded Backstrom (with Keith Tkachuk) its annual "No Guts, No Glory Honour" for his shot-blocking ability and willingness to put himself in harm's way. A highlight-reel demonstration occurred on March 4, 2010, against Tampa Bay. In a 24-second span, killing off a four-on-three penalty situation, Backstrom blocked three consecutive slapshots by Lightning defenseman Kurtis Foster, whose shot has been timed at more than 100 miles per hour, to protect a one-goal lead. "It's uplifting to teammates when a guy pays the price like that,"

said Capital Brooks Laich. "Especially when it's one of your stars."

Backstrom signed a lucrative long-term deal — 10 years for $67 million — in spring 2010, with Ovechkin in the third year of a 13-year contract. "I was thinking that I wanted to play with him," Backstrom said, pleased at the thought of lining up with an elite winger through the heart of his NHL career. "Hopefully he'll want to play with me, too.... I think it's good that we're together."

"I never for one minute, with Alex Ovechkin or Nicklas Backstrom, think that they won't compete all the way through," said Washington general manager George McPhee, explaining why he wasn't worried about his players slacking off after becoming multi-millionaires. "It sends the right message to our fans and to this franchise that we have outstanding young players who are ready to commit for the rest of their career. You win championships with these kinds of players."

STATS:

	GP	G	A	Pts	PIM
RS	323	87	236	323	160
PO	37	12	20	32	18

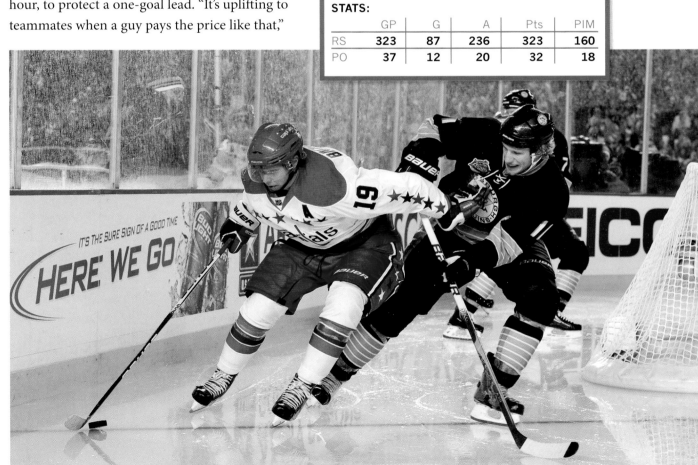

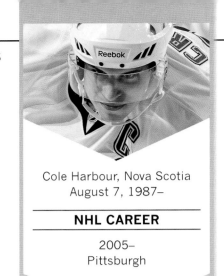

Cole Harbour, Nova Scotia
August 7, 1987–

NHL CAREER

2005–
Pittsburgh

SIDNEY CROSBY

"There can't be a better way to end the tournament than having a guy like that score the winning goal," noted Team Canada's Jonathan Toews. "It gives it a real storybook feel, for sure."

Such has been the hockey life of Sidney Crosby, who had just scored in overtime to give Canada the gold medal at the 2010 Olympic Games. He has been a game-changer since he first laced up skates. When the Pittsburgh Penguins were the winners of the Crosby draft lottery in 2005, the fortunes of a club that had just flirted with bankruptcy immediately looked bright.

"I've won the Stanley Cup, won gold medals," said Pittsburgh's former general manager Craig Patrick. "Getting Sidney Crosby was the happiest day of my life."

The NHL's lockout season of 2004–05 had put a bigger spotlight on junior hockey. Crosby, nationally known since he was 10 years old, was the Canadian Hockey League's Player of the Year for both the 2003–04 and 2004–05 seasons, playing for the Rimouski Oceanic in the Quebec League; during the latter he posted a 66-goal, 102-assist season.

With the burden of expectation on his shoulders, 18-year-old Crosby suited up for the 2005–06 season with the Penguins. "I'm not trying to be the next Wayne Gretzky or Mario Lemieux," said Crosby. "I am putting pressure on myself to do my best and perform to my potential — that's all I can do."

"He thinks about hockey 24 hours a day," said team owner Mario Lemieux, who boarded Crosby with his family for five years. "Even in his sleep it seems."

Although Crosby was edged out by the dynamic Russian Alex Ovechkin, almost two years his senior, in Calder Trophy voting, "Sid the Kid" notched an impressive 39 goals and 63 assists in his rookie season, besting Lemieux's Pittsburgh record for first-year players, and finished sixth in league scoring.

More help arrived in Pittsburgh through the entry draft, notably centers Evgeni Malkin, Jordan Staal and goalie Marc-André Fleury. Still only 19, Crosby led the league in scoring during the 2006–07 campaign, with 36 goals and 84 assists, becoming the youngest player in NHL history to win the Art Ross Trophy. The Penguins made the playoffs for the first time since 2001, but they lost in the first round. Crosby was awarded the Hart Trophy, the Lester B. Pearson Award and a First All-Star Team berth for his exceptional season. Those accomplishments were then topped off by Pittsburgh making him team captain.

He missed a lot of action with a high-ankle

AWARDS: 1st All-Star, 2nd All-Star, Hart, Pearson, Richard, Stanley Cup

STATS:

	GP	G	A	Pts	PIM
RS	412	215	357	572	387
PO	62	30	52	82	36

sprain the following season, but Crosby still scored 72 points in 53 games. Mid-season, he signed a five-year $43.5-million contract extension, taking him through the 2012–13 campaign with the Penguins. Healthy in time for the playoffs, Crosby and the Penguins marched to the Stanley Cup final. They lost to a powerful Detroit club, with Crosby and Red Wing Henrik Zetterberg, the Conn Smythe Trophy winner, finishing tied for the playoff lead, with 27 points.

Crosby concluded 2008–09 third in league scoring (Malkin won the title), with 33 goals and 70 assists, and the Penguins once again met Detroit for the Cup. Somehow Pittsburgh managed to tie the series 2–2 after losing the first two games, but when Detroit won the next game 5–0 it seemed the Penguins were spent. However, a gritty 2–1 victory evened things up, and then the Penguins managed to win the seventh game in another 2–1 nail-biter.

"Everything it took to win, we did it," said an exultant Crosby, the youngest NHL captain to ever raise the Stanley Cup in victory. "Blocking shots. Great goaltending. Different guys stepping up. I mean, we did exactly everything it takes to win. We're really happy with the result. We've been through a lot."

In 2009–10, in addition to his mid-season Olympic heroics, Crosby tied Tampa Bay's Steven Stamkos as the league's top goal-scorer during the regular season, with 51 goals, and the two shared the Maurice Richard Trophy.

"He has become a focal point of hockey in our country," said Hockey Canada president Bob Nicholson at the 2010 Olympics. "Going in, we had a lot of superstars on our team, but we only had one Sidney Crosby."

On a league-leading scoring tear in 2010–11, including a 25-game point streak, Crosby was felled by a couple of marginally legal hits that led to a concussion. His prolonged absence provoked a deeper discussion about how to prevent head injuries, as many echoed Nicholson's sentiments. Everyone looks forward to future years, when "Sid the Kid" will have outgrown his nickname.

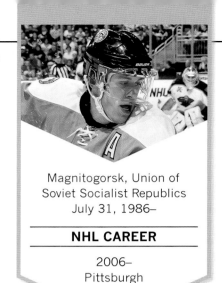

EVGENI MALKIN

Magnitogorsk, Union of
Soviet Socialist Republics
July 31, 1986–

NHL CAREER

2006–
Pittsburgh

It took a little longer than the Pittsburgh Penguins wanted, but Evgeni Malkin's NHL debut was worth the wait. Drafted at 18 years of age in 2004, right behind fellow Russian Alex Ovechkin, Malkin was forced to honor a contract with Metallurg Magnitogorsk, a team in the Russian Superleague, which he had first joined as a 17-year-old. He didn't get to Pittsburgh until the 2006–07 campaign, but when he finally arrived Malkin set an NHL record by scoring in each of his first six games, amassing seven goals and four assists before being shut out for a match. "We knew he was a great talent, but not to that extent," gushed Pittsburgh co-owner Mario Lemieux. "From what I've seen so far, he's going to be a great player for many years to come." Prescient as usual, Lemieux has watched Malkin remain a dominant force in the league.

At 6-foot-3 and 195 pounds, Malkin didn't have Ovechkin's heft, but he demonstrated extraordinary balance, a long reach and soft hands around the net. On the strength of 33 goals and 52 assists, with a number of them coming as a winger for Sidney Crosby, Malkin earned the Calder Trophy as top rookie. He credited Crosby for showing him the work ethic needed for NHL success. As a sophomore in Pittsburgh, Malkin helped lift the Penguins to second place in the

regular season despite Crosby's 28-game absence. Malkin finished second in league scoring behind Ovechkin, with 47 goals and 59 helpers, earning the First All-Star Team berth at center. He was also runner-up for the Hart Trophy and helped take the Penguins to the Stanley Cup final, where they lost to Detroit in six games. As a key member of a young club, "Geno" Malkin was rewarded the following summer with a five-year contract extension worth $43.5 million.

It's an almost impossible challenge to be the best player on the ice when you play with Sidney Crosby, but Malkin often manages to accomplish just that. In the 2007–08 season, when Crosby was out for an extensive period with an ankle injury, Malkin stepped up his game. "His confidence level is higher this year," said teammate Sergei Gonchar, a fellow Russian who had taken Malkin in as a rookie who spoke no English and given him a place to live for almost three years. "His English is better," noted

AWARDS: 1st All-Star (2), Calder, Ross, Smythe, Stanley Cup

STATS:

	GP	G	A	Pts	PIM
RS	352	158	260	418	356
PO	62	29	44	73	89

Gonchar, explaining how Malkin had overcome a tendency to go through peaks and valleys of intensity. "He has his own house, his family is with him, so I guess his comfort level is higher."

Malkin won the Art Ross Trophy with a career-best 113 points in 2008–09, thanks in large part to an NHL-best 78 assists and 35 goals. Malkin also became the first player to lead both the regular and post-season scoring derby since Lemieux in 1992. Malkin's 14 goals and 36 points were the highest playoff point total since Wayne Gretzky tallied 40 in 1993, and his stellar effort made him the first Russian to be awarded the Conn Smythe Trophy. More importantly, he helped his Pittsburgh teammates raise the Stanley Cup after defeating the Red Wings in a nail-biting seven-game final. Once again, Malkin lost the Hart Trophy to Ovechkin, but, like most players, he wouldn't have traded his Cup ring for the entire NHL trophy case.

On the international stage, Malkin captained Russia to a gold medal at the 2004 World Under-18 Championship. While gold has eluded him since, Malkin is a regular member of Russia's teams. He even pulled triple duty in 2006, playing in the World Junior Championship, the Winter Olympics and the World Championship.

After Malkin tied a career high with a five-point night in a December 2010 game versus Phoenix, Sidney Crosby said of him, "He was playing unbelievable. It's really fun to see a teammate take over a game like that and when he is playing like that, I think he pushes everyone to raise their level. I was just trying to keep up with him and make sure that I was there to create things when he was open."

"For Sidney Crosby to shake his head a bit and 'wow' is a unique thing," noted Pittsburgh coach Dan Bylsma. But the rest of the hockey world looks at Malkin with awe on a regular basis. His skill and creativity are sure to draw gasps of astonishment for years to come.

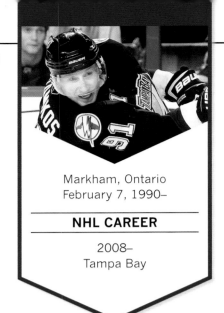

STEVEN STAMKOS

Markham, Ontario
February 7, 1990–

NHL CAREER

2008–
Tampa Bay

He was a "can't miss" kid through school and junior hockey, but Steven Stamkos has continually honed a diligent work ethic that has helped propel him further and faster than even his most die-hard fans could have predicted. Born in Markham, Ontario, just outside of Toronto, he showed unusual natural ability at a young age. "Steven could do things at five that kids 10 years old couldn't do," noted his former coach Paul Titanic. "He was saucering passes and putting shots under the crossbar. It was hard to believe to watch him at that age."

But Stamkos had parents who stressed education, understanding the precarious nature of a future built only on athletics. In high school, despite scoring 105 goals and 197 points in the 2005–06 season for the Markham Waxers and being drafted first into the Ontario Hockey League, Stamkos maintained full dedication to his studies. He notched 100 goals and 197 points over two seasons with the OHL's Sarnia Sting and was also named the league's top student-athlete in 2006–07. "He brought the same qualities he had on the ice to the classroom," said Stamkos' grade 12 English teacher, Trevor Weir. "He was driven and determined to do very well. He wouldn't accept mediocrity."

Stamkos began 2008 by winning a gold at the World Junior Championship with Canada, just a few months before the Tampa Bay Lightning selected him first overall in the NHL draft.

While Stamkos had always faced some detractors (he was rather small and scrawny before having a large growth spurt in his teens), his coach with the Lightning expressed doubts that his highly touted 18-year-old should be playing in the NHL. Barry Melrose had become the Bolts' bench boss in 2008–09 after more than a dozen years in the broadcast booth following his first coaching gig with the LA Kings. He severely limited Stamkos' ice time and was fired 16 games into the season. Melrose defended himself stating, "Steven is going to be a good player.... Right now he's just not strong enough physically to play against defensemen who are 6-foot-3 or 6-foot-4 that can skate as well as him."

It wasn't until about midway through the campaign that Stamkos started to look like he truly belonged. He notched a hat trick against Chicago in mid-February and scored 19 points in his last 20 games of the season. Although he received next to no consideration for Rookie of the Year honors, at the end of the campaign he had a very respectable 23 goals and 23 assists on a sad-sack team that had posted a league-low 24 victories.

Stamkos represented Canada at the 2009 World Championship and scored seven goals and four assists in just nine games. Although Canada lost a nail-biter finish to Russia, Stamkos came home with a silver medal and renewed confidence.

However, his best move was accepting an invitation to work and train at the home of one of hockey's warhorses over the summer. Alongside the recently retired Gary Roberts, briefly a Lightning teammate and widely admired for his dedication to nutrition and fitness, Stamkos immediately felt benefits. Six days a week, Roberts guided him through a workout routine designed to develop more core and lower body strength, which would enhance his speed and stability on the ice. Catered organic meals completed the program. "Not the best tasting food," laughed Stamkos. "But then the adjustment takes place in your body, and you can feel how healthy you're eating." The benefits really showed when the 2009–10 season got underway.

Stamkos completed an outstanding sophomore campaign, and requests to work with Roberts came pouring in from other players.

AWARDS: 2nd All-Star, Richard

STATS:

	GP	G	A	Pts	PIM
RS	243	119	113	232	151
PO	18	6	7	13	6

Although the Lightning failed to make the playoffs again, Stamkos potted 51 goals and tied Sidney Crosby for the league lead. Only Wayne Gretzky and Jimmy Carson have had a 50-goal season at a younger age. Stamkos also led his team with 95 points, clicking exceptionally well with veteran Martin St. Louis, another creative playmaker. In 2010–11, Stamkos picked up right where he had left off, challenging for the league scoring title pretty much from the first game. "When he's on the ice, you're just praying he's not around the puck," said Pittsburgh general manager Ray Shero about Stamkos. "He's got great speed, a great release, an unbelievable shot — he is a really, really dangerous player. There are only maybe a handful of guys like that in the league." High praise for a player who is just 21, but observers seem to agree that Stamkos is the real deal.

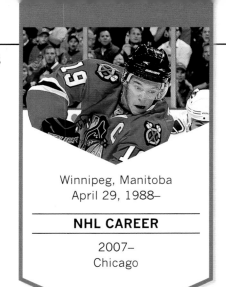

Winnipeg, Manitoba
April 29, 1988–

NHL CAREER

2007–
Chicago

JONATHAN TOEWS

Hockey players aren't really known for taking a creative approach when tagging teammates with nicknames, but members of the Chicago Blackhawks were right on the money when they dubbed their young leader, Jonathan Toews, "Captain Serious." A few other appropriate monikers might be "Mr. Everything" and "Johnny Success." When you consider everything Toews has achieved in his career, both in the NHL and on the international scene, his résumé sparkles. When you consider he turned just 23 in April 2011, his résumé is staggering.

Most hockey fans got their first formal introduction to Toews while he was representing Team Canada at the 2007 World Junior Championship. Dueling against future Blackhawks teammate Patrick Kane and Team U.S.A. in the tournament semifinal, Toews took advantage of an International Ice Hockey Federation rule that allows players to make multiple attempts in the shootouts and scored three times to push Canada to the final, where they won gold. Considering what was at stake and the fact that he went three-for-three on his attempts, Toews' showing might just be the best clutch shootout performance by a skater in hockey history.

Later that spring Toews, who was attending the University of North Dakota at the time, represented Canada at the men's World Championship, becoming just the fifth Canadian, and the first in more than 20 years, to skate in both the World Junior Championship (WJC) and Worlds in the same season. Far from a young kid tagging along, Toews chipped in seven points in nine games, becoming the first Canadian player to strike gold at both the World Juniors and Worlds during the same year. He could almost have retired before playing a single NHL game and still have been considered a hockey legend.

Drafted third overall in 2006, Toews was finally ready to make his NHL debut with the Blackhawks in the 2007–08 season. His first game became extra special when he scored his first big-league goal in the first period, even though the team lost that season-opener to the San Jose Sharks. After the game, Toews' comments demonstrated to Blackhawks fans exactly what their young rookie was all about. "It was a great moment," Toews told the Associated Press, "but the bigger picture is the game tonight, and I was disappointed not to come out on top."

Toews went on to record a point in his first 10 games that season, finishing with 54 in an injury-shortened 64-game regular season. Kane slid in to claim the Calder Trophy as Rookie of

AWARDS: Smythe, Stanley Cup
STATS:

	GP	G	A	Pts	PIM
RS	302	115	152	267	168
PO	46	15	31	46	32

the Year, and, with its two young stars, a Chicago franchise that had struggled both on the ice and at the gate suddenly seemed relevant again.

After narrowly missing the playoffs in 2007–08, the Blackhawks took a huge step forward by advancing all the way to the Western Conference final in 2009 before losing to the mighty Red Wings. Prior to that campaign, Toews was handed the "C" in Chicago, becoming the youngest captain in team history and the third youngest in NHL history, at 20 years and 79 days old.

Some thought Chicago might slip following their appearance in the final four, as young teams often take a step backward at some point. However, 2009–10 would be a dream season for both the Blackhawks franchise and its unquestioned leader. Before the business of chasing a Stanley Cup took place, Toews once again donned the red and white and played for Canada at the 2010 Olympics in Vancouver.

While Sidney Crosby eventually scored the "golden goal" to secure an overtime win over Team U.S.A. in the final, Toews led Team Canada with eight points in seven games and posted a stellar plus-9 rating, earning himself "top forward" honors at the Games.

True to his no-nonsense nature, Toews was able to put the high of Olympic gold behind him and focus on the playoffs. The Blackhawks entered the post-season as second seed in the West and advanced to the Stanley Cup final by sweeping number-one-ranked San Jose, after having knocked off Nashville and Vancouver in the first two rounds. Facing a tough Philadelphia Flyers squad, the Blackhawks were able to squeeze out a victory when Kane scored the overtime winner in Game 6 to bring Chicago its first Stanley Cup since 1961. Toews, who finished second in playoff scoring, with 29 points in 22 games, took home the Conn Smythe Trophy as post-season MVP. With all that hardware on his shelf, "Captain Serious" wore a smile of satisfaction a mile wide.

WINGERS

LEGENDS

Mike Bossy 56

John Bucyk 58

Charlie Conacher.............................. 60

Mike Gartner 62

Bernie Geoffrion.............................. 64

Gordie Howe 66

Bobby Hull.. 68

Brett Hull.. 70

Jaromir Jagr 72

Jari Kurri.. 74

Guy Lafleur 76

Ted Lindsay...................................... 78

Frank Mahovlich 80

Dickie Moore.................................... 82

Maurice Richard.............................. 84

MIKE BOSSY

Montreal, Quebec
January 22, 1957–

NHL CAREER

1977–87 NY Islanders

A goal-scorer's paradise, the Quebec junior leagues are notorious for sacrificing defense in favor of offense. Nevertheless, it was astonishing that Mike Bossy had averaged 77 goals a year over four seasons with the Laval Nationals. More surprising was that Bossy was still available in the 1977 NHL entry draft when the up-and-coming New York Islanders made their first selection.

That Bossy went 15th that year did nothing to diminish his confidence. After signing his first NHL contract, he predicted a 50-goal rookie season. Since Buffalo's Rick Martin had set the rookie scoring record six years earlier with 44 goals, Bossy's prediction sounded like a naive boast. He admitted later that even he was surprised when he shattered the record with a 53-goal campaign. He won not only the Calder Trophy, but a prestigious Second All-Star Team selection at right wing as well.

An extraordinary goal-scorer, Bossy was perhaps the greatest sniper in league history. He had an incredibly quick release with his wrist shot and could score from anywhere in the offensive zone. His accuracy was uncanny at even the toughest angles, but he was most deadly in the slot. Bossy became an integral part of the young and increasingly successful Islanders franchise, combining with center Bryan Trottier

and left winger Clark Gillies on a powerhouse line right from the beginning. Bossy followed up his rookie year with 69 goals, a career high but no fluke. His 10 NHL seasons were remarkable for his accomplishments and his consistency, and he had five seasons with 60-plus goals. Only in his last year, when the ailing back that forced his early retirement in 1987 hobbled him for most of the season, did he fail to score at least 50 goals (he still tallied 38).

Bossy set himself a lofty personal goal at the start of the 1980–81 season: He set out to score 50 goals in 50 games, an achievement matched only by the legendary Maurice "Rocket" Richard in 1944–45. Bossy started the season in fine form, but he needed two more goals in his 50th game, at home against the Quebec Nordiques. Quebec managed to keep him off the scoreboard until, with just over four minutes remaining, the mighty Islander power play took the ice. Bossy banged in

AWARDS: 1st All-Star (5), 2nd All-Star (3), Byng (3), Calder, Smythe, Stanley Cup (4), HHOF 1991

STATS:

	GP	G	A	Pts	PIM
RS	752	573	553	1,126	210
PO	129	85	75	160	38

a goal after a scramble in the crease, and the air of anticipation that had marked the night became almost electric.

Bossy got one more miraculous chance when Trottier found him unguarded and snapped a pass over with a minute and a half left in the game. Bossy rifled home his 50th. He finished the season with 68 goals and a First All-Star Team selection, his first. He then led all playoff goal-scorers on his way to his second Stanley Cup. In all, he won four Cups with the Islanders, making a significant contribution with 61 playoff markers in those four consecutive years, including the Cup-winning goals both in 1982, when he won the Conn Smythe Trophy, and in 1983.

Because of his elegant play and commitment to a nonviolent approach to the game, Bossy won the Lady Byng Trophy three times and was runner-up once. An outspoken critic of fighting and intimidation, he refused to drop his gloves even when goaded. (Of course, the presence of his linemate Gillies offered him a measure of protection.) Despite the machismo prevalent in the NHL, Bossy suffered little criticism for his convictions, and he always played his own style, exacting his revenge on the power play.

In attempting to dissuade Bossy from hovering anywhere near the net, many defensemen resorted to a cross-check to his back as a method of moving him away or slowing him down. Such cheap shots took their toll. After he retired, Bossy worked on a public campaign to educate minor hockey players about the danger of hitting from behind.

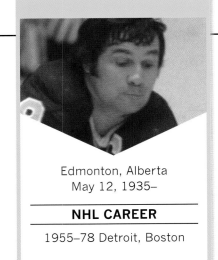

JOHN BUCYK

Edmonton, Alberta
May 12, 1935–

NHL CAREER

1955–78 Detroit, Boston

"It breaks your heart when a club lets your buddies go," said John Bucyk late in his career, "but you can't be soft about it. It's a hard game and a hard life, and you do the best you can. It's been a good life for me."

Bucyk patrolled left wing for 21 seasons in Boston, setting the club record of 545 goals, which still stands. He arrived in the 1950s, when the Bruins were serious contenders for the Stanley Cup, survived the club's eight-year era of futility in the 1960s and was a team mainstay in the glory years of the 1970s. Even after his retirement, Bucyk has remained an active and visible Bruins employee for three decades and counting. It's difficult to picture him with any other organization, yet Bucyk played his first two NHL seasons with the Detroit Red Wings.

Bucyk grew up in Detroit's farm system, and the Red Wings thought enough of the promising winger that they gave him a Stanley Cup ring as a member of their 1955 championship team, even though he didn't dress for a game. The following winter, he saw limited action in his rookie year, scoring only a single goal, and he did not distinguish himself greatly the next season. Meanwhile, Detroit general manager Jack Adams decided to bring proven goalie Terry Sawchuk back from Boston.

"Being traded for [Sawchuk] made me feel good," said Bucyk, "and it was the biggest break in my career. I wanted to play hockey more than anything, and knowing that I'd be getting regular ice time had me excited to get to Boston." Even better, Bucyk was reunited with former junior linemates Bronco Horvath and Vic Stasiuk, and the "Uke Line"— named for Bucyk's and Stasiuk's Ukrainian heritage — skated together for four productive seasons.

One of the heaviest forwards in the league for most of his career, Bucyk packed 220 pounds on his 6-foot frame and used his bulk to his advantage, banging into the corners and parking himself at the opposition net. "I never knew anyone who could hit a guy harder," noted Bobby Orr, "especially with a hip check."

Bucyk was an integral part of the "Big Bad Bruins," but he confined his aggressiveness to legal hits. "I know the Lady Byng isn't a popular trophy with the Boston fans," he said in 1970,

AWARDS: 1st All-Star, 2nd All-Star, Byng (2), Stanley Cup (2), HHOF 1981

STATS:

	GP	G	A	Pts	PIM
RS	1,540	556	813	1,369	497
PO	124	41	62	103	42

after finishing as runner-up for the award for the second time, "but I'd sure like to win it." Bucyk's wish came true when he combined a career-high 51 goals and 65 assists with a meager eight minutes in penalties the following season. He took the Byng again in 1974 and finished just behind Marcel Dionne in 1975.

Bucyk was nicknamed "Chief" because some fans thought he looked Native American, but others may have assumed the title referred to his leadership position on the club. Bucyk was first named team captain in the fall of 1966, but he found his off-ice responsibilities too time-consuming and suggested he share the load. Bucyk traded his "C" for an "A." The captainless Bruins competed for six years with as many as four alternates, but when the team won the Stanley Cup in 1970 and 1972, there was no doubt about who would raise the victory mug first.

While Bucyk hit the 50-goal plateau only once (just the fifth player at the time to do so), he was a consistent scorer. "If you're going to get goals," he explained, "you've got to get in where the action is." His hard-nosed style wasn't flashy, but he joined the 500-goal club in 1975.

"I've hit more posts than nets," he said, "but the numbers are nice. I've thought of myself as a spear-carrier, not a star, really.

I've just gone along getting what I could out of every game, and it's added up."

The Bruins officially retired Bucyk's No. 9 sweater when he retired in 1978.

CHARLIE CONACHER

Toronto, Ontario
December 20, 1909–
December 30, 1967

NHL CAREER

1929–41 Toronto, Detroit,
NY Americans

Although some decried Toronto's Jesse Ketchum Park as a breeding ground for juvenile delinquents, hockey scouts kept a close eye on the ice rinks there. Amid a plethora of card and crap games, there was always at least one hockey game in progress, and the neighborhood hangout spawned a number of NHL players, Charlie Conacher among them. The poverty that surrounded him fueled Conacher's desire to make a career of professional hockey. "It represented money," he said. "We didn't have a pretzel. We didn't have enough money to buy toothpaste."

The Maple Leafs signed Conacher into their organization in 1929, having seen his potential and bloodlines. Conacher's brother Lionel, nine years his senior, was already beginning to establish the family name as one of the greatest in Canada's sporting history.

Lionel "Big Train" Conacher was voted Canada's best athlete of the half-century in 1950, but he was a hero in his brother's eyes long before that. Following in Lionel's footsteps, Charlie excelled at every sport he tried, particularly football, baseball, lacrosse and hockey. When Charlie saw his brother make the professional hockey ranks, he made sure his skating was top-notch. By the time Charlie had worked his way up to the Toronto Marlboros in junior hockey,

Lionel had already played two NHL seasons for the Pittsburgh Pirates and was on his way to New York to play for the Americans.

When the younger Conacher graduated to the Maple Leafs in 1929, he scored 20 goals in his rookie year. One of the NHL's heftiest players, at 6-foot-1 and just under 200 pounds, Conacher was a sharpshooter with heavy ammunition. "It felt like somebody had turned a blowtorch on me," said Ottawa defenseman King Clancy after blocking one of Conacher's wrist shots. "I couldn't sit down for a week."

Conacher led the league in goals in his second season, a feat he accomplished four more times in the next five years. Charlie "The Big Bomber" Conacher had earned his own nickname and a chance to replace Ace Bailey on Toronto's best line.

When coach Conn Smythe united Conacher with "Gentleman" Joe Primeau and Harvey "Busher" Jackson (the term busher referred to a go-getter), Toronto's original "Kid Line" was born. The combination was dynamite: Conacher again scored the most goals in the 1931–32 season; Primeau, the Lady Byng winner, had the most assists for the second consecutive year; and Jackson won the scoring crown with the most points. Their line maintained a torrid

AWARDS: 1st All-Star (3), 2nd All-Star (2), Stanley Cup, HHOF 1961

STATS:

	GP	G	A	Pts	PIM
RS	459	225	173	398	523
PO	49	17	18	35	49

pace through the playoffs, vanquishing Lionel Conacher and his Montreal Maroons in the semifinals. The Big Bomber continued to hit the target and led his team in goals and points — assisting on the clinching tally — to help the Maple Leafs defeat the New York Rangers and win their first Stanley Cup in Maple Leaf Gardens in 1932.

Conacher made the Second All-Star Team, and the next season (1932–33), he and Lionel were both named to the second squad. One season later, both brothers cracked the First All-Star Team. Charlie won his first scoring title, with 32 goals and 20 assists, while Lionel was steering the Chicago Black Hawks to a Stanley Cup victory. The two met head-to-head in the league final for the first and last time in the spring of 1935, both in pursuit of their second Stanley Cup championship. Charlie had already won the scoring race again, and Lionel was back with the Montreal Maroons, who swept the Maple Leafs in three straight games.

Conacher had one more All-Star season just ahead of him, but injuries took their toll thereafter. He played only 34 games over the next two regular seasons, after which the Maple Leafs sold him to the Detroit Red Wings. Although Conacher starred for the Red Wings in the 1939 playoffs, he was traded that summer to the New York Americans. He put in two undistinguished years before retiring in 1941, at the age of 31.

After coaching junior hockey for several years, Conacher was hired to coach the Black Hawks in 1947. His younger brother, Roy, was his best player and won the Art Ross Trophy as scoring champion in 1949. Conacher retired from coaching a year before his son Pete, the next member of hockey's "royal family," made it to the NHL, in 1951.

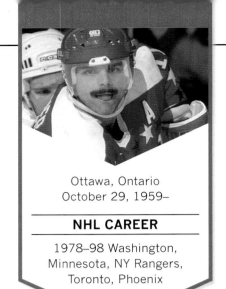

Ottawa, Ontario
October 29, 1959–

NHL CAREER

1978–98 Washington,
Minnesota, NY Rangers,
Toronto, Phoenix

MIKE GARTNER

Filling in for injured teammate Mark Messier at the 1993 All-Star Game, Mike Gartner not only won the skating race in the NHL All-Star Skills Competition, but he also took away a car as the prize for being named the game's most valuable player. Opening the scoring with two goals only 22 seconds apart on his way to a first-period hat trick, Gartner contributed a fourth goal in the second period, helping the Wales Conference set an All-Star Game–scoring record in a 16–6 blowout. "I'll give Mark a big handshake," he laughed when asked whether he owed Messier anything, "but not the car!"

Gartner was the quietest member of a select group. On December 15, 1997, he became only the fifth NHL player to register 700 goals in a career. Like Gordie Howe, another "700 Club" member, Gartner never erupted for a 60- or 70-goal season, but he did hit the prestigious 50-goal mark in the last game of the 1984–85 season. The key to Gartner's success was consistency. He holds the NHL record with 17 seasons of 30 or more goals, with 15 of those seasons in succession. The lockout-shortened 1994–95 season interrupted his unprecedented streak, but trades never broke his stride. Gartner is the only player who has scored 30 or more goals for five different teams.

In 1978 Gartner made a bold move when he signed as an underage free agent with the WHA's Cincinnati Stingers. When the NHL swallowed the rival league the next year, the Washington Capitals made Gartner the league's number-four draft pick. Generous amounts of ice time on a weak Washington team translated into more goals than even Gartner knew he was capable of scoring. Although convinced that his strength lay in his two-way play, Gartner found his niche as a fleet sniper. "My speed was a God-given thing," he said. "I worked on it, but for the most part, it was there from the very beginning, when I was a kid." He established franchise records for career goals and points (since bettered by Peter Bondra), but after 10 years with the Capitals, Gartner was traded for the first time in March 1989 to the Minnesota North Stars.

Although Gartner tallied more than a point a game for Minnesota, he was sent to the New York Rangers a year later. He had three

	GP	G	A	Pts	PIM
RS	1,432	708	627	1,335	1,159
PO	122	43	50	93	125

AWARDS: HHOF 2001
STATS:

consecutive 40-goal years in Manhattan. The 1991–92 season was an especially auspicious one: He recorded his 500th goal, 500th assist and 1,000th point and played in his 1,000th NHL game. All cylinders were firing as the Rangers headed toward their first Stanley Cup victory in over 40 years, but at the 1994 trade deadline Gartner was dealt to the Toronto Maple Leafs. Gartner never played on a Stanley Cup winner.

Gartner completed two solid seasons for the Maple Leafs before he was sent to Phoenix. The 36-year-old proved he still had wings when he won the NHL skating race for the third time at the 1996 All-Star Game. "You knew if you got him the puck, he could make things happen," said Larry Murphy, who played with Gartner in Washington, Minnesota and Toronto. "When

you played against him, you had to respect his speed. You had to back off him or he'd burn you." But Gartner battled injuries in 1997–98, for the first time in his career, and Phoenix didn't renew his contract.

Gartner had free-agent status, but he honored a commitment he had made to his wife and children — to be settled at that point in their lives. "Maybe I'm leaving something on the table," he said in announcing his retirement, "but 20 years from now, will it matter if I scored 780 goals instead of 708? Will it matter if I played 22 years instead of 19?" Gartner bowed out gracefully and took up a full-time position with the NHL Players' Association. He was inducted into the Hockey Hall of Fame in 2001, and the Washington Capitals retired his No. 11 in 2008.

BERNIE GEOFFRION

Montreal, Quebec
February 16, 1931–
March 11, 2006

NHL CAREER

1950–64, 1966–68 Montreal,
New York Rangers

Bernie Geoffrion invented the slapshot in his youth, and when he brought it to the big leagues, it was unlike anything the NHL had ever seen. "It's definitely harder than anything [Charlie] Conacher shot," claimed Toronto coach Hap Day, who played with Conacher in the 1930s. "I watched Geoffrion closely on one play. I saw him draw the stick back, but I didn't see the puck until it bounced off the goalpost."

Geoffrion's nickname, "Boom-Boom," referred to the sound of the puck reverberating off the end boards, but he hit twine often enough that the Montreal Canadiens were clamoring for his services while he was still a teenager. He had joined Montreal's junior team at the age of 14 and more than held his own, and he continued to improve his entire game while paying particular attention to the shot that would make him famous. Geoffrion held out until there were only 18 games left in the Canadiens' 1950–51 season, potting eight goals but still preserving his rookie status for the following year. He then won the coveted Calder Trophy, with 30 goals and 24 assists.

Geoffrion had a glorious career with the Canadiens; his name went on the Stanley Cup six times. He scored more than 20 goals in a season a dozen times for Montreal — when that total really meant something in the NHL. Unfortunately, Maurice Richard (who also patrolled right wing for Montreal), Detroit's Gordie Howe and Andy Bathgate of the Rangers were such outstanding players that it was difficult for Geoffrion to gain league-wide recognition for his considerable talents. Even after Geoffrion won the scoring championship in the 1954–55 season, Richard was named to the First All-Star Team. Geoffrion's resulting anger, however, was nothing compared to that of the fans in the Montreal Forum when Richard was suspended for the last few games of the season and Geoffrion passed him to earn the scoring title by a single point.

"I couldn't deliberately not score," complained Geoffrion, but the boos and catcalls rained down on him regardless. "I was sick of the whole thing," an emotional Geoffrion later confessed. "Even thinking about hockey made me throw up. I wanted to get away from hockey. But [Jean] Beliveau and [Maurice] Richard visited me. They urged me to stay in the game."

Even after Richard retired in 1960 and Geoffrion won his second Art Ross Trophy in 1960–61 — with only the second 50-goal campaign in NHL history — some fans continued to harbor resentment that Boom-Boom had again entered Richard's territory.

However, the season did end happily: Most of the Forum gave Geoffrion a standing ovation, he made the First All-Star Team and he earned the Hart Trophy as the league's MVP.

Geoffrion called it quits after the 1963–64 season. He then coached minor league teams in the Canadiens organization for two years. When the step up the ladder he believed he had been promised didn't materialize, he severed his long relationship with Montreal.

Geoffrion arrived in New York in 1966, although not as coach. He made a remarkable comeback and reentered the NHL ranks as a player with the Rangers. He helped the team make the playoffs twice — he never missed the playoffs for over 16 seasons in total — before

deciding to retire for good in 1968.

He briefly coached the Rangers and then the Atlanta Flames for their first few seasons in the early 1970s, and he made a celebrated but short-lived return to Montreal in 1979. But his nerves and personality weren't suited to coaching. Geoffrion returned to Atlanta and eventually helped his adopted hometown regain an NHL franchise.

AWARDS: 1st All-Star, 2nd All-Star (2), Calder, Hart, Ross (2), Stanley Cup (6), HHOF 1972

STATS:

	GP	G	A	Pts	PIM
RS	883	393	429	822	689
PO	132	58	60	118	88

GORDIE HOWE

Floral, Saskatchewan
March 31, 1928–

NHL CAREER

1946–71, 1979–80
Detroit, Hartford

Affectionately known as "Mr. Hockey," Gordie Howe is the most durable and consistent star ever to lace on skates. Not only did he play 26 NHL seasons, he dominated the league for most of that time. In his 23rd NHL season, he reached his highest point total of 103. For 20 consecutive years, he finished among the top-five scorers in the league, and he garnered 21 All-Star team selections. In today's game, he would be regarded as a power forward, but his teammates simply called him "The Power."

On the ice, Howe deferred to no one. Detroit general manager Jack Adams had to pull him aside after his first three NHL seasons and point out that he needn't have a punch out with every player in the league. Howe curbed his fighting, which seemed to translate directly into more goals, but he remained one of the nastiest players in the game. He was just subtler about it.

Howe had a rare ambidextrous shooting ability, but he also possessed the sharpest elbows in the league. "We had very poor equipment and I have very sloping shoulders," he has explained. "It was almost a necessity to get my elbow out." But Howe wasn't opposed to wielding his stick as a weapon either, and he used his awesome strength in surprising ways. "When a guy was a little faster than me and we were going behind

the net," he once laughed, "I'd swing a little wide to give him the inside spot, then squeeze him off so he'd run into the net. A lot of guys have told me, 'Oh, I knew when I was halfway through there, I was in trouble.'"

While Howe notched only seven goals as a rookie, he impressed the Red Wings enough to be placed on a line with slick Sid Abel and feisty sniper Ted Lindsay in his second season. Before long, the "Production Line" was tearing up the league. After losing the Stanley Cup final two years in succession, Howe tried to ram Toronto's Ted Kennedy into the boards in the first game of the 1950 playoffs. Kennedy ducked, and Howe crashed into the boards headfirst. Rushed to hospital, for a while it looked as if he might not live through the night. In time, Howe made a full recovery.

The early 1950s were Detroit's glory years (four Stanley Cups in six seasons), and although the Cup eluded him thereafter, Howe maintained his personal excellence through thick and thin. Still racking up points but suffering constant pain with arthritis, he retired in 1971. At the age of 43, Howe moved into a front-office executive position. He hated it, desperately wanting to be more than a ribbon cutter. So in 1973, when the newly formed WHA invited him to join his young sons Mark and Marty on a line for the Houston Aeros, he jumped at the chance. Howe was an All-Star again and added 174 goals and 334 assists to his career totals. Howe regarded the six seasons spent playing with his boys in the WHA the highlight of his 33 years in professional hockey.

Despite hints of disappointment at having his NHL career goal-scoring record broken by Wayne Gretzky, Howe has always maintained an amiable relationship with Gretzky, who has idolized Howe since he was a boy. The last time their paths crossed in a meaningful way on the ice was in 1980, when Gretzky played in his first NHL All-Star Game and Howe played his last. The loyalties of the 21,000 fans in Detroit's Joe Louis Arena were loud and clear. "I didn't know what to do with myself," Howe admitted later, as it seemed the standing ovation for him would never end. "It's still hard to accept appreciation. I'd love to show that I accept this with a great amount of gratitude, but how do you do it?" A few months later, at age 52, Howe hung up his skates for good.

AWARDS: 1st All-Star (14), 2nd All-Star (9), Hart (6), Ross (6), Stanley Cup (4), HHOF 1972

STATS:

	GP	G	A	Pts	PIM
RS	1,767	801	1,049	1,850	1,685
PO	157	68	92	160	220

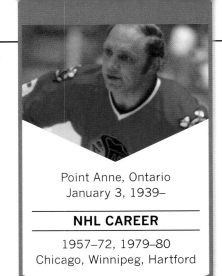

Point Anne, Ontario
January 3, 1939–

NHL CAREER

1957–72, 1979–80
Chicago, Winnipeg, Hartford

BOBBY HULL

"The Golden Jet" electrified NHL audiences for 15 seasons with his tremendous speed, muscular good looks and unprecedented goal-scoring ability. "You knew what he was going to do — you could read him like a book," maintained Gordie Howe, "but he was so strong, he'd do it anyway."

And yet, all that power was tempered by good grace. "Always keep your composure," advised Bobby Hull, who won the Lady Byng Trophy in 1965. "You can't score from the penalty box; and to win, you have to score." While Hull owns only one Stanley Cup ring, he had no shortage of goals and wins during his career. In 1965–66, he became the last NHL scoring champion to win with more goals than assists, and for seven seasons he led the league in goals scored.

An outspoken critic of violence in hockey, Hull even staged a one-man, one-game strike during the 1977–78 season to publicize his cause. Yet he systematically terrorized opposition goalies, cranking noisy shots off the glass during warm-ups and publicly discussing his strategy of firing his first shots in a game at the goalie's head. Netminder Gump Worsley challenged Hull bare-faced over 15 seasons — maintaining Hull only talked of firing the hard, high one and, instead, rifled in a low shot — but most goalies were instinctively back on their heels.

When his teammate Stan Mikita started experimenting with a curved stick in the early 1960s, Hull joined him in tinkering with the new weapon. The "banana blade" was born, and Hull was thrilled with the results. "If you don't quite catch all of the puck as you let it go, it'll rise or drop suddenly, depending on the spin," he explained in 1966. "Drawing it toward you as you let it go sets up a different spin that produces a curve."

With 54 goals in the 1965–66 season, Hull broke the long-standing record of 50 goals in a season (he'd previously matched the records of Maurice Richard and Bernie Geoffrion); the following season, he tallied 52 goals. Toronto netminder Johnny Bower complained, "He needs another shot like I need a hole in the head, which I may get."

In 1967, the NHL stepped in with a new rule limiting a stick's curve, and when Hull broke his own record in 1968–69 with 58 goals, the league further limited the curve. Yet it would be a gross overstatement to claim that the hooked blade was the key to Hull's success. Many experts believe he would have scored more than 70 goals in 1968–69 without the big curve, suggesting it impeded his accuracy.

Hull's career scoring record is impressive. He

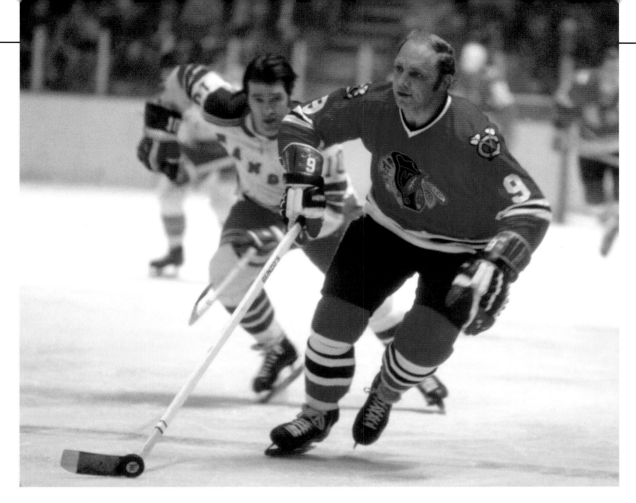

won the Art Ross Trophy three times, and of the 10 first 50-goal seasons, five were his. Although he left the Chicago Black Hawks while still in his prime, he holds most of that franchise's career goal-scoring records.

Hull rocked the hockey world when he signed with the Winnipeg Jets of the upstart WHA in 1972. Every franchise ponied up to give Hull a million-dollar signing bonus on top of the Jets' record-breaking salary offer, and Hull (who had initially made an outrageous demand just to get the WHA to leave him alone) felt compelled to accept the lucrative deal. "If I told you the big

contract had nothing to do with my signing," he admitted after, "I'd be lying." But he cited a long-standing complaint about how Chicago had negotiated with him over the years. Almost immediately, every professional hockey player was able to command more money — if a living legend such as Hull could jump to the new league, who else might?

Hull added 303 goals and 335 assists in just over six WHA seasons, most as a left winger on a line with the elegant Swedes Anders Hedberg and Ulf Nilsson. He retired from hockey in the fall of 1978, but he made a brief comeback to the NHL when the Jets joined the league in 1979. Shortly after being traded, Hull ended his career after nine games with the Hartford Whalers, hobbled by injuries. Hull's No. 9 jersey was eventually raised to the rafters in both Winnipeg and Chicago.

AWARDS: 1st All-Star (13), 2nd All-Star (4), Byng, Hart (2), Ross (3), Stanley Cup, HHOF 1983

STATS:

	GP	G	A	Pts	PIM
RS	1,063	610	560	1,170	640
PO	119	62	67	129	102

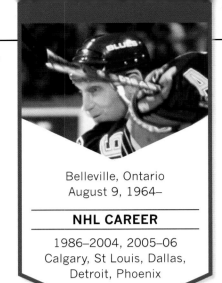

Belleville, Ontario
August 9, 1964–

NHL CAREER

1986–2004, 2005–06
Calgary, St Louis, Dallas,
Detroit, Phoenix

BRETT HULL

"I'm a goal-scorer," said Brett Hull. "That's not all I do, but that's what I do best." Hockey scouts were always convinced about Hull's sniping skills, but they were less certain about whether he could play at the NHL level. As the son of Hockey Hall of Fame–legend Bobby Hull, "The Golden Jet," Brett naturally attracted attention when he closed out his teenage years by tallying 105 goals as a Junior B player. But at that age, his father had been rifling in goals for the Chicago Black Hawks.

"Maybe I've got his genes, but I definitely don't have his personality," said Brett. "You're talking to the laziest man alive. I'm not into expending physical energy. I'm into expending mental energy. On the ice, my dad was like a thoroughbred. I'm more like a train. I chug."

The Calgary Flames decided to risk their sixth draft pick and made Hull the 117th player chosen in 1984. He also earned an invitation to the University of Minnesota at Duluth, where he potted 84 goals in 90 games over two seasons. A year with Moncton in the AHL followed, and on the strength of 50 goals and 42 assists, he got the long-awaited call-up to the Flames in the spring of 1987.

Doubts about his work ethic persisted, even through his official rookie season (1987–88),

when he tallied 26 goals and 50 points in 52 games. The Flames made a trade — debatable even then — dealing Hull to the St. Louis Blues in 1988. The move soon looked downright foolish.

Hull maintained his solid scoring pace with the Blues, contributing seven playoff goals in 10 games and leading his new club with 41 goals and 43 assists in the 1988–89 season. However, he made magic happen the following year. Newly acquired center Adam Oates, one of hockey's slickest passers, helped "The Golden Brett" score 72 goals, a record for a right winger. Hull shattered his own mark with 86 goals in the 1990–91 season and added 70 more the year after. Only Wayne Gretzky has ever found the net more often over a three-season span.

In addition to making the First All-Star Team three times running, Hull was awarded the Lady Byng Trophy in 1990 and the Hart Trophy and Lester B. Pearson Award in 1991. "My whole game is based on deception," he explained. "I'm there, and then I'm not. I don't want to be noticed. I barely raise my arms when I score. I don't want people mad at me for making them look stupid."

Hull's production slowed over his next half-dozen seasons with the Blues, yet he still scored an average of more than 40 goals a year.

He endured a lengthy feud with coach Mike Keenan, who ultimately lost the public battle and was fired. Hull has always been unafraid of controversy. He angered league officials by complaining about the interference he and other finesse players faced nightly. "It's not the referees' fault," said Hull. "It's the people above them. They're ruining the game. It's embarrassing. I wouldn't pay money to watch that. The game's going to hell in a handbasket."

Hull signed a free-agent contract with Dallas in July 1998 and hit two milestones with the Stars: "It's a weird feeling," he said. "You hope to get one goal in this game, but to say I have 500 goals and 1,000 points is a thrill. I'll long remember this night." Hull capped a memorable season by scoring the 1999 Stanley Cup–winning goal in overtime.

After three seasons in Dallas, Hull joined the Detroit Red Wings for 2001–02 and sipped again from the Cup at the end of the season. He surpassed his father's 610 career NHL goals in 2000 and notched his 700th goal in February 2003. After the NHL lockout of 2004–05, Hull struck a deal with the Phoenix Coyotes, but he retired after only five games.

Hull's sweater number was retired by St. Louis in 2006, but later that year he took a management position with the Dallas Stars, where he has served in several roles. In 2009, he was inducted into the Hockey Hall of Fame.

AWARDS: 1st All-Star (3), Byng, Hart, Pearson, Stanley Cup (2), HHOF 2009

STATS:

	GP	G	A	Pts	PIM
RS	1,269	741	650	1,391	458
PO	202	103	87	190	73

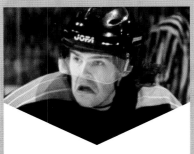

JAROMIR JAGR

Kladno, Czechoslovakia
February 15, 1972–

NHL CAREER

1990–2004, 2005–08, 2011–
Pittsburgh, Washington,
NY Rangers,
Philadelphia

Although the wild mane of curly hair that spilled onto his shoulders from beneath his helmet has been gone for years, Jaromir Jagr may be best remembered as the rebellious youth who roared onto the NHL scene in 1990. He was a spectacular sight, tearing down the ice with the puck seemingly tied to his stick with a string. His boyish good looks added to his charm, yet his juvenile attitude diminished his accomplishments at times. His military salute after scoring — a tribute, he maintained, to his grandfather — was seen by most opponents as a cocky taunt. Jagr wore No. 68 in memory of the same grandfather, who died in a Czechoslovakian jail as a political prisoner in 1968.

Born in 1972, four years after Soviet Union tanks rolled in to strengthen a threatened communist government, Jagr came of age during his homeland's next uprising. Fortunately, the "Velvet Revolution" wasn't quashed, and Jagr became the first hockey player from his country to attend an NHL draft without having to defect. The Pittsburgh Penguins picked him early in the first round of the 1990 NHL entry draft.

Someone soon discovered that Jaromir was an anagram for "Mario Jr.," and, indeed, Jagr seemed cut from the same cloth as team captain Mario Lemieux. At 6-foot-2 and 230 pounds, he has Lemieux's reach, strength and stickhandling ability. His 27 goals and 30 assists in his rookie year helped the Penguins finish first in their division, and he contributed 13 playoff points toward Pittsburgh's first Stanley Cup victory in 1991. The following year, he was a dominant factor in defending the Cup, scoring 11 goals and 13 assists in the playoffs.

"There's so much innocence to him," said veteran Gordie Roberts in 1992. "He enjoys everything. He hasn't realized yet that hockey is a business."

During Lemieux's season off to convalesce from Hodgkin's disease, Jagr edged out Eric Lindros to take the 1994–95 scoring title. Lemieux returned the following year, and Jagr erupted with his most productive season, scoring 62 goals and 87 assists. He finished second to Lemieux in the race for the Art Ross Trophy.

"You always want to score a beautiful goal," said Jagr. "That's what you're trying to do. Score some goals like that, get more confidence for the other ones." Yet his scoring crown in 1997–98 came on the strength of his league-leading 67 assists. One of the most artistic and creative players of all time, Jagr also barges to the net, drawing hooks, slashes and power-play opportunities.

"Playing with him is a lot of fun," said Stu

Barnes in 1998. "You never know what you're going to see next. But he's also a guy who really works hard off the ice, and that's something he doesn't get enough credit for." With Lemieux in retirement, Jagr was given the team captaincy in the summer of 1998, when Ron Francis left the team through free agency.

He was scoring champ again in 1998–99 and 1999–2000, and he won a fifth Art Ross Trophy, with a 52-goal and 69-assist campaign, the following season. Unfortunately for Pittsburgh fans, the franchise's financial woes prompted trades of most of the team's high-priced talent. Jagr was dealt to the Washington Capitals, who signed him to a long-term $11-million-per-season contract in the summer of 2001.

He led the Capitals in 2001–02, with 79 points in 69 games, and again in 2002–03, with 77 points. But Washington, too, went on a cost-cutting spree, and the Caps dealt Jagr to the NY Rangers in the middle of the 2003–04 season.

He vied for the NHL scoring title again in 2005–06, and Jagr was given the Lester B. Pearson Award by his peers for the third time. He was named team captain and continued to post respectable scoring numbers, yet Jagr's desire seemed to wane at times in New York. When the Rangers didn't offer him a contract for 2008–09, Jagr spurned other NHL enquiries and joined the KHL, Russia's professional league, for three seasons before signing a one-year deal with Philadelphia for the 2011–12 campaign.

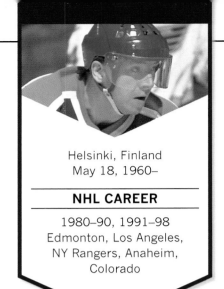

Helsinki, Finland
May 18, 1960–

NHL CAREER

1980–90, 1991–98
Edmonton, Los Angeles,
NY Rangers, Anaheim,
Colorado

JARI KURRI

"There was a tremendous load off the back of the entire team," admitted Jari Kurri after the Edmonton Oilers won the Stanley Cup in 1990, "because we demonstrated that we weren't a one-man show." Kurri, who earned his fifth Stanley Cup ring with that win, probably felt more relief than anyone else on the Oilers team. When Wayne Gretzky was sold to the Los Angeles Kings in 1988 — the two had been the dominant offensive pairing of the 1980s — many said Kurri would be ordinary without him. Kurri proved his critics wrong. In his first NHL season without Gretzky, Kurri made the Second All-Star Team with a 44-goal, 58-assist campaign. During the 1990 Stanley Cup playoffs, he scored 10 goals and added 15 assists.

While Gretzky was at the peak of his offensive power in Edmonton, Kurri made more of a contribution than was sometimes acknowledged. Gretzky himself is always the first to credit his teammates for his success, and no one was closer

to Gretzky than Kurri. In the end, the two played 13 seasons together. "We see the game the same way," said Gretzky. Coming from "The Great One," this is a generous compliment. The two seemed to operate on an intuitive level: Kurri found his way to open ice, Gretzky found him with the puck and Kurri had the soft hands to finish the play. He also made great passes; his 797 career assists are proof that he was a premier playmaker too.

Kurri was also more than just an offensive force. He was runner-up to Bobby Clarke in voting for the 1983 Selke Trophy, and it's surprising Kurri never won that award as the league's best defensive forward. Perhaps his offensive numbers threw the voters off. Assigned to Gretzky's line after a number of players had auditioned, Kurri knew from the start that two-way play would be critical to his success. He earned league-wide respect for his clean defensive play (he is a Lady Byng Trophy winner), but he still had six 100-point seasons. Kurri had a career year in 1984–85, setting a new high for right wingers with 71 goals and finishing with 135 points. He led the league with 68 tallies the following season.

Still, Kurri somehow managed to save his best hockey for the playoffs. He was the leading

AWARDS: 1st All-Star (2), 2nd All-Star (3), Byng, Stanley Cup (5), HHOF 2001

STATS:

	GP	G	A	Pts	PIM
RS	1,251	601	797	1,398	545
PO	200	106	127	233	123

playoff-goal-scorer four times — the Oilers won the Cup on each occasion — and he shares a record with Philadelphia's Reggie Leach for 19 goals in one post-season. Kurri's two overtime markers, seven hat tricks and 10 shorthanded scores lifted him to third place on both the all-time playoff goals and points lists at the end of his career.

A contract dispute in 1990–91 led to a year of play in Italy before a three-team trade sent Kurri to the Los Angeles Kings. Reunited with Gretzky for two seasons, he helped the Kings to the 1993 Stanley Cup final. He was traded to the New York Rangers in 1996.

Kurri's defensive game had become his primary contribution, and he bounced to several teams before finishing his career in 1997–98 with the Colorado Avalanche. Shortly after notching his 600th career goal, he played for the World Team (players born outside North America) at the 1998 All-Star Game. Kurri scored a goal, but Gretzky slipped a pass by him to Mark Messier, who scored the game-winner for the North American side. "Wayne still fools even me," laughed Kurri. "I told him at the faceoff: 'I back-check all those years for you, and that's how you treat me?' "

In 2001, Kurri became the first Finnish player to enter the Hockey Hall of Fame. The Edmonton Oilers retired his No. 17 sweater the same year.

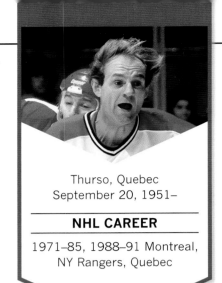

Thurso, Quebec
September 20, 1951–

NHL CAREER

1971–85, 1988–91 Montreal,
NY Rangers, Quebec

GUY LAFLEUR

When he got the puck on his stick, the Montreal Forum crowd came alive with cries of "Guy! Guy!" The fans edged forward in their seats, anticipating at least an exciting play, if not a goal, and the focus of their attention, Guy Lafleur, rarely disappointed.

Heralded as a franchise player when he was drafted by the Montreal Canadiens in 1971, Lafleur began his career with a heavy responsibility. Many saw him as a replacement for the legendary Jean Beliveau, who had retired the same year. Lafleur had created high expectations with an extraordinary junior career, tallying 130 goals and 79 assists in his last season with the Quebec Remparts.

While Lafleur's rookie NHL campaign was excellent by normal standards (29 goals and 35 assists), he followed it up with seasons of 55 and 56 points and was frequently portrayed by the media as a disappointment. In truth, Montreal boasted an incredible lineup and intentionally broke in rookies slowly.

Lafleur finally had a breakthrough in the 1974–75 season, with 53 goals and 66 assists, and many cited the fact that he doffed the helmet he had worn for his first three seasons as a factor. Whether or not having the wind blow through his hair made Lafleur feel more creative

and reckless, as some claimed, it certainly wouldn't have been quite the same for the fans if he'd had a helmet on. As he danced and whirled up the ice, "The Flower" was a beautiful sight, and Lafleur became a huge box-office draw as the first player to have six consecutive 50-goal and 100-point seasons.

Induction into the Hockey Hall of Fame represents the pinnacle of a successful hockey career. A player basks in the spotlight, while he and others reflect on his accomplishments and past glories. Not so for Lafleur. In 1988, while others were fondly looking back at his three scoring championships and five Stanley Cup victories with the Montreal Canadiens, Lafleur was anxiously looking ahead. He was only days away from finding out whether he could skate his way back into the NHL after three years of unsatisfactory retirement.

Lafleur's attempt at a comeback caught most fans totally off guard. But his retirement in 1985

AWARDS: 1st All-Star (6), Hart (2), Pearson (3), Ross (3), Smythe, Stanley Cup (5), HHOF 1988

STATS:

	GP	G	A	Pts	PIM
RS	1,126	560	793	1,353	399
PO	128	58	76	134	67

had not been freely chosen. Although, in 1978, Lafleur had described hockey as being "like a dream to me," by 1984 it had become a nightmare. Former teammate and then coach Jacques Lemaire imposed a tightly controlled defensive system that stifled Lafleur's natural gifts. Since Lafleur's game was offense, he saw a decreasing amount of ice time, which is poison to any scorer. Soon, some of the fans were starting to get on his back because, even when he got on the ice, Lafleur showed little of his famous flash and creativity. Handcuffed by Lafleur's stature, team management ignored his appeals for a trade, so he quit in frustration. For three years, he missed the game terribly.

When the New York Rangers beckoned with the offer of a tryout in 1988, Lafleur proved that he could still play in the NHL. He had a decent season, with 18 goals and 27 assists, and played two more seasons after that with the Quebec Nordiques. Age was finally catching up with him though and his performance was only average, but Lafleur had succeeded in proving to himself and to everyone else that he could have been a contributing player during his forced "sabbatical."

When Lafleur finally announced his forthcoming retirement in 1991, on his terms, he received an appreciative acknowledgment from every crowd in every city, but especially in Montreal. All past indignities and disputes were buried, and Lafleur later happily took an off-ice job as one of the Montreal Canadiens' exalted ambassadors.

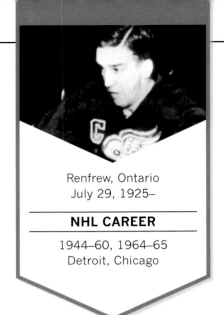

TED LINDSAY

Renfrew, Ontario
July 29, 1925–

NHL CAREER

1944–60, 1964–65
Detroit, Chicago

Detroit hockey fans can thank Lady Luck for making Ted Lindsay a Red Wing. After Lindsay played well in his first game for Toronto's St. Mike's junior team, the Maple Leafs brass was alerted that the school had a rookie forward the Maple Leafs should consider. At a subsequent game, the Toronto scouts put the best forward they saw on the ice on their "protected" list, making him Leafs' property. Unknown to them, however, this forward was not Lindsay — he had been knocked out of the lineup with a severe gash in his leg.

When the still-hobbled Lindsay resumed playing, he attracted little notice. By January he was fully healed and showing the feisty vigor for which he would become legendary. In 1944, the day after a game against Detroit's junior affiliate, Lindsay was signed by the Red Wings organization.

"Terrible" Ted Lindsay was short of stature and temper. He eventually retired as the most penalized player of all time. Lindsay played a mean game, and the damage he inflicted often led to bloody retaliation, as indicated by the 700 stitches he took in his face during his career. But the league's most hated player earned nothing but appreciation in Detroit.

"He's the guy who holds us together," claimed Sid Abel, the center of the famous "Production Line" between Lindsay and Gordie Howe. "He keeps us at a high pitch. He won't allow anyone to let down when he's on the ice."

Lindsay commanded respect off the ice as well. "It was all in the tone of his voice," said Howe. "It was very authoritative."

Lindsay wasn't hesitant about taking initiative. He captained the Red Wings to a Stanley Cup victory in 1954. After the final game, the Stanley Cup was placed on a table at center ice, and the winning team stood around it drinking champagne — but Lindsay had a different idea. "It was an impulsive sort of thing," he later explained. He hoisted the Cup over his head and skated a lap around the ice near the boards to give the jubilant fans a better look. A tradition was born.

"As long as the fans don't boo you at home, you don't have to worry," he said in 1957. "If they boo you on the road, you must be doing something to help your own club. As for the other players, I'd like them all to be my friends — off the ice." The latter admission reflected a new approach because in previous years, Lindsay admittedly "hated" his opposition all the time. But the injustices he saw inflicted, especially on less successful players, inspired him to form a Players' Association in 1956. Secret

AWARDS: 1st All-Star (8), 2nd All-Star, Ross, Stanley Cup (4), HHOF 1966

STATS:

	GP	G	A	Pts	PIM
RS	1,068	379	472	851	1,808
PO	133	47	49	96	194

meetings were held until January 1957, when the first Players' Association press conference stunned league owners. Their rage was eventually vented on all the key figures.

Despite the distraction of his off-ice activity, Lindsay enjoyed his most productive NHL season in 1956–57, tallying 30 goals and 55 assists, but the following summer he was dealt to the cellar-dwelling Chicago Black Hawks — as close to exile as existed in the NHL at that time — along with the outspoken young goalie Glenn Hall. Toronto's Conn Smythe sent his troublemakers to Chicago as well, and the threat of further retaliation against the Players' Association killed Lindsay's organization effort.

In the spring of 1960, Lindsay retired from

hockey and returned to Detroit. He made a brief but successful one-season comeback in 1964–65, after Sid Abel became Detroit's general manager. "Emotionally," said Lindsay, "I'd never left." He served the Red Wings as general manager himself in the mid-70s, and the club officially retired his No. 7 sweater in 1991. In 2010 his legacy to the game grew even greater. The NHL Players' Association announced it was renaming the Lester B. Pearson Award — given to the outstanding player in the regular season, as decided by the players themselves — the Ted Lindsay Award.

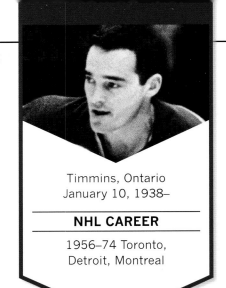

Timmins, Ontario
January 10, 1938–

NHL CAREER

1956–74 Toronto,
Detroit, Montreal

FRANK MAHOVLICH

Few superstars have been unappreciated for as long as Frank Mahovlich, who spent nearly 11 years in a love-hate relationship with the Toronto Maple Leafs. Mahovlich burst onto the NHL scene in the 1957–58 season, edging out Bobby Hull in Calder Trophy voting for Rookie of the Year. The Maple Leafs managed to get to the Stanley Cup final the following two seasons, but the team's new savior couldn't quite take them to the promised land. That all looked to change when Mahovlich erupted with 38 goals in the first 35 games of the 1960–61 season. He eventually set the club record with 48 goals at season's end, but he was seen by some as a disappointment. A pattern had been set.

"No one else is so elegant, so electric, so furious, so fluid," wrote Peter Gzowski in 1961. "Other skaters stride, he swoops. They glide, he soars. They sprint, he explodes." But Toronto's coach and general manager, Punch Imlach, wanted his team to dominate through defense and rigid positional play. While Mahovlich scored dozens of beautiful goals in helping the Maple Leafs win three consecutive Stanley Cups in 1962, 1963 and 1964, the autocratic Imlach encouraged Mahovlich — and the fans and media — to believe there should have been dozens more goals.

"If Toronto fans would appreciate his great talent and give him the cheers he deserves instead of booing him," said Gordie Howe in the mid-60s, "maybe the pressure wouldn't cook the guy." The soft-spoken Mahovlich suffered two nervous breakdowns and was sent to hospital both times with a diagnosis of deep depression and tension.

At the end of the 1964–65 campaign, Andy Bathgate, who was a creative winger like Mahovlich, said: "Imlach never spoke to Frank Mahovlich or me for most of the season, and when he did, it was to criticize. Frank usually got the worst. We are athletes, not machines, and Frank is the type that needs some encouragement, a pat on the shoulder every so often." That outspoken observation was Bathgate's last as a Maple Leaf, but "The Big M" remained in Toronto for several more years.

Mahovlich sipped champagne from the Stanley Cup for a fourth time in 1967, before the Maple Leafs made a blockbuster trade late in the following season that sent him to the

AWARDS: 1st All-Star (3), 2nd All-Star (6), Calder, Stanley Cup (6), HHOF 1981

STATS:

	GP	G	A	Pts	PIM
RS	1,181	533	570	1,103	1,056
PO	137	51	67	118	163

Red Wings. The Maple Leaf Gardens switchboard was swamped with outraged callers, but for Mahovlich: "It was as if a piano had been lifted off my back." His production improved dramatically, and he hit a career high of 49 goals in 1968–69 on a line with Gordie Howe and Alex Delvecchio.

After two All-Star seasons, Mahovlich was traded to the Montreal Canadiens in 1971. "Hockey is fun again with this bunch," he admitted with a grin. "Even in practices, you can feel the Canadiens' love of sheer speed and what has become known as firewagon hockey." Mahovlich jelled immediately with his new teammates and found the net 14 times in the spring of 1971 to set a playoff goal-scoring record and help the Canadiens win the Stanley Cup. He followed up with his two highest regular season point totals on the way to Montreal's Stanley Cup victory in 1973, before he was lured back to Toronto. This time, however, it was to play for the Toronto Toros of the World Hockey Association.

Mahovlich spent four years in the WHA, the last couple with the Birmingham Bulls in Alabama, which made for a rather ignominious end to a Hockey Hall of Fame career. But the rewards have come. In 1998, Mahovlich, with his hockey celebrity his only obvious qualification, was appointed by Liberal Prime Minister Jean Chretien to the Canadian Senate. He can hold the unelected position until age 75.

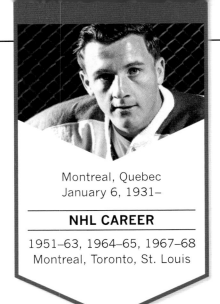

Montreal, Quebec
January 6, 1931–

NHL CAREER

1951–63, 1964–65, 1967–68
Montreal, Toronto, St. Louis

DICKIE MOORE

Dickie Moore was upset, wondering whether he was holding back his linemates by playing with a broken wrist. His centerman, Henri "The Pocket Rocket" Richard, looked as if he had a real shot at the 1957–58 Art Ross Trophy as scoring leader. On the other wing, the legendary Maurice "Rocket" Richard was still an offensive force and as fiery a personality as ever. When Moore offered to relinquish his spot on the line, Montreal coach Toe Blake called a meeting and asked the Richard brothers whether they wanted a change.

"We got here together," they quickly replied, "we end together." That vote of confidence, Moore believed, typified the attitude of the Montreal Canadiens in the 1950s. In the end, Moore did prevent Henri Richard from winning the scoring crown that year, but only because he took it home himself.

Three months with a specially designed cast helped Moore suit up for every contest that season, and he missed surprisingly few games over his years with Montreal, despite myriad other injuries. For all his formidable talent, Moore was fortunate even to have made it to the NHL. Two broken legs as a boy marked the beginning of a lifetime plagued with knee problems. Although hampered by numerous operations, separated shoulders and broken

hands, wrists and collarbones, and more than the average number of stitches, bruises and sprains, Moore never really stopped.

He followed up his Art Ross–winning campaign by setting a new record while defending his title the following year. His career-high 41 goals and 55 assists would not be beaten for seven seasons. Moore also made a huge contribution to six Stanley Cup victories for Montreal, including all five consecutive wins in the last half of the 1950s.

His team boasted eight future Hockey Hall of Fame members, and it took Moore some time to feel comfortable in that milieu. "It was like a nightmare for me as a young player," he admitted, "being around some of those great hockey players."

Moore had worked his way up through the Canadiens organization, but, unwilling to sign for the NHL's minimum salary, Moore didn't join the parent club until Christmas 1951. He then scored an impressive 18 goals in the 33 games remaining in his rookie season with the Canadiens, but injuries restricted him to only 31 NHL games — and three goals — over the next two seasons. Healthy through the 1953 playoffs, he contributed three goals to Montreal's Stanley Cup win. He then led all scorers in post-season action the following year, aided by a record-breaking two-goal, four-assist game.

"The worst thing that could happen to a hockey player is that he starts to think," Moore once said. "A hockey player is not smart enough to think." Yet, his obvious intelligence added a dimension to his rugged approach to the game, and he resented the notion that he was uncontrolled. "I did anything I had to do to win and keep my job," he explained with self-awareness. "I had to play a certain style."

In 1962, Moore started an equipment-rental company, a venture that met with the disapproval of the Canadiens' brass, who thought it would distract him from hockey. When Montreal initiated conversations about trading him in 1963, Moore quit hockey. "I couldn't think of playing for someone else," he claimed, although Toronto managed to lure him back to the NHL for the 1964–65 season, after one year of retirement. Still only 33 years old, Moore was restricted by injuries to 38 games, and his two goals and four assists convinced him that it was time to hang up his skates again.

When the league expanded in 1967, the St. Louis Blues persuaded Moore to come out of retirement one last time. Again limited by injuries, he played only 27 games but showed flashes of his former glory and helped his team to the Stanley Cup final. While his team bowed out to Montreal in four straight games, Moore made his final exit with his head held high, distinguishing himself with seven goals and seven assists in 18 playoff games. In 1974, he was inducted into the Hockey Hall of Fame.

AWARDS: 1st All-Star (2), 2nd All-Star, Ross (2), Stanley Cup (6), HHOF 1974

STATS:

	GP	G	A	Pts	PIM
RS	719	261	347	608	652
PO	135	46	64	110	122

Montreal, Quebec
August 4, 1921–
May 27, 2000

NHL CAREER

1942–60 Montreal

MAURICE RICHARD

Rarely does a man gain mythic status while he is still alive, but early in his career, Maurice Richard transcended the role of folk hero. While the goals he battled for were on the rink, "The Rocket" seemed to personify many of the aspirations and frustrations of French Canada. Nothing illustrated that relationship so well as the explosive night of March 17, 1955, in what became known as "The Richard Riot."

Two days earlier, Richard had been involved in a stick-swinging brawl. His explosive energy, best exemplified by his flashing dark eyes, occasionally expressed itself in rage. Disarmed of his stick three times in a raucous melee, Richard committed the unpardonable sin of striking a linesman with his fist. NHL president Clarence Campbell suspended the Montreal star for the final few games of the season as well as for the playoffs.

At the time, Richard was leading the NHL scoring race and the Canadiens were vying with the Detroit Red Wings for first place, so Montreal fans felt that the rug had been pulled out from under them. Campbell was the target of numerous threats, but he took his regular seat at the next Canadiens home game. On arrival, he was pelted with insults, eggs and debris. The Canadiens were soon losing to Detroit by

a 4–1 margin, and the crowd grew angrier Someone lit a tear-gas canister as the first period ended, and Campbell forfeited the match to Detroit.

The enraged fans streamed out of the Montreal Forum, joining several thousand others outside who were demonstrating against Richard's suspension. An estimated 5,000 people then went on a rampage, smashing windows and looting stores in downtown Montreal. The next day, while shopkeepers cleaned up the mess, Richard went on the radio and appealed, successfully, for calm.

Many have argued that the Richard Riot was the dawn of Quebec's Quiet Revolution, signaling an end to French-Canadian tolerance of English-Canadian subjugation. Regardless, it was a defining moment for Richard, the Montreal Canadiens and the NHL. The Canadiens lost to Detroit in seven games in the Stanley Cup final that year, but they went on to win five consecutive Cups before the Rocket retired in 1960 and Montreal's remarkable streak ended.

Richard's record of 50 goals in 50 games, set during the 1944–45 season, stood until Mike Bossy equaled his achievement in 1981. Richard broke Nels Stewart's long-standing record of 325 regular-season goals and set a new high of 544 career goals before hanging up his skates.

Yet he is best remembered for his playoff performances. Perhaps the ultimate clutch player, Richard scored six playoff overtime goals, long an NHL best and only surpassed by Joe Sakic's eight. His 82 playoff tallies included 18 game-winners, four hat tricks, two four-goal games and a five-goal barrage against the Toronto Maple Leafs on March 23, 1944. In fact, he so dominated that game — a 5–1 Canadiens' victory — that he was chosen its first, second and third star.

Richard believed there was only one thing that separated him from the pack: desire. "I had the same kind of determination from the time I was a boy of 7 or 8," he explained. "I wanted to win all the time, to score goals. That's all I had on my mind."

Richard led the NHL in goals scored over five separate seasons, but he never won the Art Ross Trophy as scoring champion. Fittingly, the NHL inaugurated the Maurice Richard Trophy in 1999 to honor the regular-season goal-scoring leader. "For generations of hockey players and fans, 'The Rocket' was the goal-scorer," declared NHL commissioner Gary Bettman. "His determination and skill symbolized the best the game has to offer."

Although Richard had a falling out with the Canadiens not long after he retired in 1960, he eventually patched things up and served the club as a goodwill ambassador for the last years of his life. Thousands of people — many of whom had never seen him play — lined the streets of Montreal to offer their final respects in May 2000.

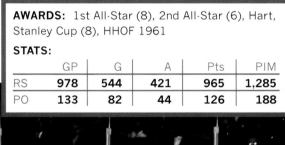

AWARDS: 1st All-Star (8), 2nd All-Star (6), Hart, Stanley Cup (8), HHOF 1961

STATS:

	GP	G	A	Pts	PIM
RS	978	544	421	965	1,285
PO	133	82	44	126	188

WINGERS
LIONS

Patrick Kane 88
Alex Ovechkin....................................90
Corey Perry 92
Bobby Ryan....................................94
Alexander Semin 96

PATRICK KANE

Buffalo, New York
November 19, 1988–

NHL CAREER

2007–
Chicago

Every player lucky enough to make it to the NHL is living the dream. However, Chicago Blackhawks star Patrick Kane is one of the very few who's experienced what every young hockey player dreams of most: the dream that begins with a shot from your stick in overtime and ends moments later with your team hoisting the Stanley Cup.

As Chicago faced a tough Flyers squad in the 2010 Stanley Cup final, the Blackhawks were attempting to end a 49-year championship drought. The Blackhawks had won three home games during the series but had dropped two in Philadelphia; if they could reverse the trend of the home side emerging victorious in Game 6, the Stanley Cup would be theirs. The visitors held a 3–2 edge on the scoreboard late in the game, but with just 3:59 left on the clock, the Flyers clawed even on Scott Hartnell's second tally of the contest.

That set the stage for a fantastic finish. The overtime period had just started, the teams were still settling in on the bench when Kane took a pass from Brian Campbell inside the Philadelphia blueline. The youngster drove to the net and fired a shot at Flyers goalie Michael Leighton from a sharp angle. The first indication the puck actually went in was Kane tossing his gloves and stick in the air behind the Flyers' net then joyously jetting down the ice to embrace his own goalie, Antti Niemi. Sure enough, Kane's shot had snuck through and was buried just inside the far post. As he waved his hands wildly, one by one his teammates realized they were now Stanley Cup winners and joined the celebration. Kane, meanwhile, joined the ranks of guys like Jason Arnott, Brett Hull and Uwe Krupp as players who had clinched championships with an overtime winner.

After the game, Kane told the Associated Press he did his best to convince everyone in the rink his shot 4:06 into the extra period had indeed ended the series. "I tried to sell the celebration a little bit," Kane said. "Everyone came down, and I think some of the guys were still kind of iffy to see if the puck was in the net."

Captain Jonathan Toews sure was. "I was just hoping to God it was just an actual goal or we would be celebrating for nothing," he said.

While Toews, the Blackhawks' other young star forward, skated off with the Conn Smythe Trophy as playoff MVP, Kane's contributions during that spring run could not be ignored. He finished the series with three goals and eight points in the final four games, bumping his post-season total to 28 points in 22 contests.

AWARDS: 1st All-Star, Calder, Stanley Cup
STATS:

	GP	G	A	Pts	PIM
RS	**317**	**103**	**200**	**303**	**142**
PO	45	20	28	48	20

That summer, Kane got to carry the Stanley Cup back home to Buffalo, where his love for hockey originally took root. Kane first emerged as a start on the U.S. national team development program's under-18 squad, then he joined the Ontario League's London Knights for the 2006–07 season. Playing on a line with a pair of other future NHLers (Edmonton's Sam Gagner and Nashville's Sergei Kostitsyn), Kane torched the league, netting 145 points in just 58 games. That June, the rebuilding Blackhawks drafted Kane first overall, one year after taking Toews with the third overall selection.

Both players debuted in the 2007–08 campaign, and while Toews' strong season was interrupted by injury, Kane played all 82 games and led the rookie scoring race with 72 points. That propelled him to top freshman honors, and he claimed the Calder Trophy.

At 5-foot-10 and 178 pounds, Kane is certainly not going to run many people over. At the same time, few players in the league are as elusive as the slippery right winger, who excels at ragging the puck in the offensive zone until the right play presents itself. Kane's hands are silky smooth, and he can fire a pinpoint shot as he is dishing the puck to an open teammate.

It has been interesting to watch Kane and Toews use their different styles to restore Chicago to its place among the league's elite teams after years in the NHL basement. Toews, a Canadian, is known for his low-key, stern approach to things, while Kane plays the part of the brash, smiling American who welcomes the accolades that come his way. The chemistry between these friends clearly works, which means Kane might once again be in a position to score a Stanley Cup–winning goal one day.

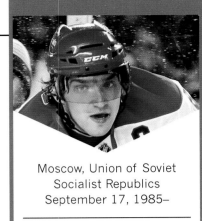

Moscow, Union of Soviet
Socialist Republics
September 17, 1985–

NHL CAREER

2005–
Washington

ALEX OVECHKIN

Alex Ovechkin is somewhat of a wild man, scruffy in appearance, gap-toothed and unusually aggressive for a sharpshooter. Always looking for opportunities to flatten the opposition, he has received numerous boarding penalties, several ejections for hitting from behind and a couple of suspensions. Yet even his foes are reluctant to call him a "dirty" player, noting Ovechkin often puts himself at equal risk of injury. "If you look at how he hits, it's all or nothing," commented Pittsburgh defenseman Brooks Orpik when Ovechkin had to sit out two games for kneeing in December 2009. "He takes 10 strides before he hits guys."

"He's a super-intense competitor," added Penguin Mark Eaton. "He brings it every shift.… But no one can be above the law."

While even Washington's coach, Bruce Boudreau, has hinted he might need to caution Ovechkin, team owner Ted Leonsis disagrees. "Alex isn't trying to hurt anyone," blogged Leonsis after the kneeing incident. "He has an honest respect for the game and for all players in the league. Alex is trying to 'get the puck.'… He plays the game the way it was designed. He is just bigger and faster than anyone. Can you name a player in NHL history that has this mix of size [6-foot-2 and 233 pounds], skill, power and speed? I can't."

Ovechkin served another two-game suspension in March 2010 for a boarding penalty on Chicago's Brian Campbell. Despite receiving a five-minute penalty and a game misconduct, as well as knowing Campbell suffered a broken clavicle and ribs (and missed six weeks of the season recuperating), Ovechkin remained unrepentant. "We play for our team, and we make some hard hits," said Ovechkin. "And sometimes, you get hurt. That's a hockey game."

"The Great Eight" burst onto the NHL scene in 2005–06, fully formed and ready for stardom. The Washington Capitals had chosen the Russian hotshot with the first pick in the 2004 NHL entry draft, then they waited expectantly through the owners' lockout of 2004–05, as their future star spent his fourth season with the famed Moscow Dynamo, which he had first joined at age 16. The son of a professional soccer player and an Olympic gold medal–winning basketball player, Ovechkin combined natural athletic ability with a rough-and-tumble attitude and competitive zeal. His NHL rookie season coincided with Canadian teenager Sidney Crosby's inaugural campaign in Pittsburgh, and both met the high expectations placed upon them, rejuvenating two tired franchises.

Similar in many respects, Crosby and

Ovechkin both exhibited prodigious scoring talent. But it was Ovechkin who earned the NHL's Rookie of the Year honors. Mid-season, he scored a goal for the ages. Checked to the ice, on his back, sliding away from the net and with one hand on his stick, Ovechkin miraculously hooked a puck that appeared to be sliding harmlessly into the corner and slid it into the Phoenix net. "That goal was one of the prettiest I've ever seen," said Wayne Gretzky, then Coyotes coach. "Guy Lafleur might have scored a few in the 1970s that were pretty remarkable, and maybe I scored a few nice ones, but not like that."

At season's end, Ovechkin had tallied a remarkable 52 goals and 54 assists, good for third place in league scoring and a spot at left wing on the NHL's First All-Star Team, a distinction he held for five consecutive years.

In 2006–07, Ovechkin tallied 46 goals and 46 assists. The following season, in the last year of his rookie contract, he signed the richest deal in NHL history — a 13-year extension for $124 million. His remarkable 65 goals (an NHL record for a left winger) and 112 points earned Ovechkin the Art Ross, Maurice Richard and Hart Trophies, as well as the Lester B. Pearson Award. In 2008–09, he retained the Pearson Award as well as the Hart and Maurice Richard Trophies, with 56 goals, and finished runner-up in overall scoring with 110 points.

The Capitals named Ovechkin team captain midway through the 2009–10 campaign, and he finished the season with 50 goals and 109 points,

AWARDS: 1st All-Star (5), 2nd All-Star, Calder, Hart (2), Lindsay, Pearson (2), Richard (2), Ross

STATS:

	GP	G	A	Pts	PIM
RS	475	301	313	614	346
PO	37	25	25	50	18

winning the newly rechristened Ted Lindsay Award (formerly the Pearson). As the most explosive, and arguably most exciting, player in hockey — and with gold medals for Russia in the World Championship, both as a junior in 2003 and at the senior level in 2008 — only consistent NHL playoff success has eluded Ovechkin to date. With the supporting cast that now surrounds him, that seems imminent, and the attempt will undoubtedly be entertaining to watch.

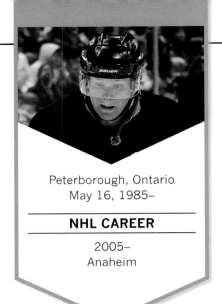

Peterborough, Ontario
May 16, 1985–

NHL CAREER

2005–
Anaheim

COREY PERRY

In his sixth NHL season, Corey Perry won the Maurice "Rocket" Richard as the NHL's top goal-scorer and the Hart trophy as the NHL's MVP, cementing himself as a premier player in the world's best league. Perry's Richard and Hart wins, however, are only the most recent triumphs in what has been nothing short of a spectacular career.

He hit junior hockey's highest heights in 2004–05, capping an outstanding four-season amateur career. He earned a gold medal as a member of Canada's team at the 2005 World Junior Championship, and he also led the Ontario Hockey League in scoring, notching a remarkable 47 goals and 83 assists during his last regular season with the London Knights. Perry concluded the playoffs with 11 goals and 27 helpers. He then went head to head against Sidney Crosby's Rimouski Oceanic, the Quebec League champions, for the national title. Perry hoisted the Memorial Cup and was the tournament's MVP, more than fulfilling the promise that had led the Mighty Ducks of Anaheim to use a first round pick to select him in the 2003 draft.

At 6-foot-3 and 210 pounds, Perry has enough heft to drive to the net with authority, and he plays "on the edge" effectively. A scrappy — some

would say chippy — winger with exceptional offensive instincts, Perry has made some enemies along the way. Receiving boos on the road is part of the job description of a power forward. Midway through the 2008–09 season, he was handed a four-game suspension for a reckless elbow to the head of Philadelphia Flyer Claude Giroux. He bumps into goalies, shoves after whistles and verbally taunts his opponents. "Create havoc and try to get people off their games," explained Perry.

His rookie NHL season was neither sensational nor disappointing, and Perry acquitted himself respectfully with 13 goals and a dozen assists in 56 games. He improved in 2006–07, with 17 goals and 27 assists, and played in the mid-season NHL All-Star Game for the first time. He also contributed some important playoff goals to help the Ducks win the Stanley Cup at season's end. With 29 goals the following season, Perry proved he truly had what it takes.

"Corey is one of the top young players in the NHL today," said Anaheim's former general manager Brian Burke when he signed Perry to a five-year $26.625-million contract extension in July 2008. "He's a true Duck, a hard-nosed goal-scorer who's difficult to play against."

"He'll go into all the dirty, tough areas to score goals," current Ducks GM Bob Murray told

AWARDS: 1st All-Star, Hart, Richard, Stanley Cup					
STATS:					
	GP	G	A	Pts	PIM
RS	450	168	201	369	537
PO	54	18	25	43	101

NHL.com correspondent Josh Brewster late in 2009. "He's not afraid. That's something you can't teach."

"I like to lead by example, but I like to talk in the dressing room, too," said Perry. "I'm not the guy who just sits there. I like to mix things up. I take pride in it. It's part of my game, going to the net and taking a bit of a beating if I have to. Somebody's got to do it. I guess I'll be that guy."

"I think it's both skills and grit," said Ducks coach Randy Carlyle, defining what makes Perry a dominant player. "He's a slippery guy around the net who can score. He makes a living in the crease and in, around and behind the net. He's one of those guys who can come out and put the puck into a lot of areas that other people can't."

Perry has definitely benefited from playing with center Ryan Getzlaf, whose career has closely paralleled Perry's. The two have matured into team leaders, and Perry is always quick to say that his linemate makes life pretty simple and that all he has to do is keep his stick on the ice. However, Perry even does some penalty-killing for the Ducks now, proving he's more than just a sharpshooter. After four years together, Perry and Getzlaf cycle the puck with a natural chemistry that earned them berths as linemates on Canada's 2010 Olympic team, where they teamed with Dallas Stars captain Brenden Morrow. In the gold-medal game, Perry scored Canada's second goal in a 3–2 overtime victory. "Whenever you can chip in, it's a great feeling," he wrote in a blog for ESPN Insider. "It was a great bounce and it sat there in the slot for a minute … so I had to bury it! Those are opportunities you don't get too often."

It seems likely, however, that Perry is on track for many more turns in the spotlight, with a red light beaming behind him.

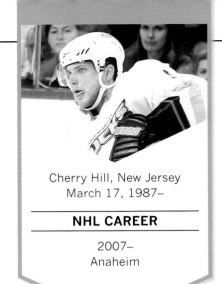

Cherry Hill, New Jersey
March 17, 1987–

NHL CAREER

2007–
Anaheim

BOBBY RYAN

With a life story that could have been lifted out of a true-crime TV show, Bobby Ryan has risen above it all to become one of the hottest young stars in the NHL. He was born Robert Stevenson in affluent Cherry Hill, New Jersey, in 1987. At 10 years of age, his family life was turned upside down and inside out. His father, Robert Stevenson Sr., an amateur boxer and successful insurance company owner at the time, came home drunk and argued aggressively with his wife. He went on a rampage, ripped a door off its hinges, chased his wife out of the house and beat her badly. Melody Stevenson spent four days in hospital with four broken ribs, a punctured lung and a fractured skull. Robert Stevenson Sr. was arrested and charged with attempted murder and five other felony counts. While out on bail, he fled to Canada. Melody Stevenson, who had forgiven him for the assault, soon joined him with young Bobby. The family was on the run, living as outlaws and moving from place to place, yet they always found ways for Bobby to pursue his passion for hockey.

The family eventually settled in El Segundo, California, just outside of Los Angeles, and Bobby joined the LA Junior Kings organization. Robert Stevenson called himself Shane Ryan and earned money as a professional gambler. Bobby

also changed his surname. "My parents made it clear," he said. "They were serious. You are Bobby Ryan, no matter who asks. No exceptions!"

Somehow, the family's wounds were healing, and Bobby Ryan's hockey team won a national title. But "Shane Ryan" made the careless mistake of renting a video with an old credit card, and in 2000 the police quickly zeroed in and arrested him. Extradition back to Cherry Hill, a guilty plea to aggravated assault and bail jumping, and a five-year jail sentence followed. "I regret it every day. This is mine for the rest of my life," said Ryan's father, now known as Bob Ryan. "Fortunately, I have two people that put me in a position to be able to make it up to them."

In 2003, Bobby Ryan joined the Owen Sound Attack of the Ontario Hockey League. Only 16 years old, he tallied 22 goals and 17 assists in 65 games, and he then erupted with 37 goals and 52 assists in 2004–05. The following summer, the Anaheim Ducks selected Ryan second overall in the NHL draft. Shortly after, Ryan decided to come clean about his alias and publicly told his story.

In 2005–06, Ryan notched up 31 goals and 95 points for the Attack before he joined the Portland Pirates of the American Hockey League for a 19-game playoff run. He concluded his junior career the next season, with 43 goals and 102 points, and he again joined Portland for the remainder of its AHL season. He became a full-time Duck in 2009–10 and tallied 31 goals and 26 assists over only 64 games, earning himself a nomination for Rookie of the Year.

Ryan's combination of size and skill — he has soft hands, excellent vision, a low center of gravity and the strength to protect the puck with his 6-foot-2, 209-pound frame — helps him cycle along the boards and set up linemates from either wing position. Skating on a line with Corey Perry and Ryan Getzlaf, a pair of stars who are just a couple of years older than him, Ryan is also a scorer. He had 35 goals in 2009–10 and added 29 assists and a silver medal for Team U.S.A. from the mid-season Vancouver Olympics to his impressive list of achievements. At season's end, the Ducks extended his contract for five years and $25.5 million.

I certainly don't have any skeletons left in my closet," noted Ryan, but he still has a few surprises left in him. In December 2010, Mikko Koivu of the Minnesota Wild lost his stick and then tried to tie up Ryan. As the two pulled apart, Koivu pulled Ryan's stick from him and skated away. Ryan, momentarily without a stick, played uncertainly for a few seconds in his own end, and then he grabbed Koivu's stick from the ice as the Ducks wheeled across their blueline. Although it was a leftie, Ryan, a right-hand shot, made the adjustment. He took a pass and deftly snapped in a goal using his opponent's stick, quite likely a first in NHL action.

STATS:

	GP	G	A	Pts	PIM
RS	250	105	97	202	181
PO	19	8	3	11	4

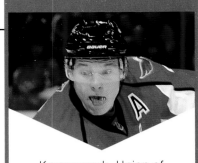

ALEXANDER SEMIN

Krasnoyarsk, Union of
Soviet Socialist Republics
March 3, 1984–

NHL CAREER

2003–04, 2006–
Washington

Alexander Semin isn't the number-one star in Washington, but the Capitals are thankful to have the slick Russian on their roster. The Capitals drafted Semin 13th overall in the 2002 draft, and after one more year of playing in his home country, the talented left winger joined Washington for the 2003–04 season, netting 10 goals and 22 points in 52 games.

The Capitals were a sad-sack team at that point, having finished with just 59 points, which tied them with Pittsburgh for the second-lowest total in the league. However, things started to turn around for the team when they won the NHL's draft lottery, enabling them to take Ovechkin first overall in June 2004. The owners' lockout that wiped out the entire 2004–05 NHL season delayed Ovechkin's arrival in Washington, but circumstances beyond labor strife kept Semin away longer than the team had hoped. After spending the lockout year in Russia, Semin spent an additional season overseas, under somewhat murky circumstances, as he fulfilled his military service. The Capitals had hoped he would play his second NHL campaign that year, but instead they had to wait until 2006–07. He was worth the wait.

Semin scored 38 goals and 73 points that year, as he and Ovechkin got the Capitals back on the road to respectability. During the next campaign,

with skilled Swede Nicklas Backstrom now on board, the Capitals made the playoffs for the first time in three seasons, and they haven't missed the post-season since. Washington has reformed its game to be more defensive, but the team still relies heavily on its high-end skill, which Semin most definitely contributes to. Though not as fast as Ovechkin, Semin shoots the puck just as hard and just as quickly. He's especially lethal when at the point on a power play. The Capitals will often work the puck around the offensive zone in the hopes of sliding it to Semin at the top of the slot so he can unload a booming one-timer.

As he gained more experience, Semin became increasingly dangerous on the ice. In the spring of 2008, he was a major factor on the Russian team that claimed World Championship gold by beating Canada on its home soil. Semin was an offensive catalyst for the Russians, scoring six goals and 13 points in nine games. He took a big step forward the following NHL season, when he recorded 79 points despite being limited to 62 games because of injury. His 1.27 points-per-game clip that year was sixth best in the league, one spot behind Pittsburgh Penguins megastar Sidney Crosby. The next season, Semin managed to hit the 40-goal barrier in 73 games, and his 84 points ranked him 13th in NHL scoring.

Unfortunately for Semin, injuries have been a common theme throughout his NHL career. On four occasions he's been limited to 65 games or less in a single season, and he has yet to dress for a full 82-game schedule, which is a shame because the Capitals are a much tougher team to stop when he's in the lineup. While Backstrom and Ovechkin often face the best checking line and defense pair the opposition has to offer, Semin can exploit a seam, using his silky hands to create goals from nowhere.

Semin was eligible to become an unrestricted free agent in the summer of 2010, following his 40-goal campaign, but he signed a one-year deal to stay in Washington. With the ability to test the open market again during the 2010–11 season, Semin once more opted to re-sign for another single season. With a number of star players already drawing monstrous salaries, it's tough for Capitals GM George McPhee to make room for Semin long-term, but both the team and the player appear happy to maintain their relationship. "Players who score like this are rare, they're really hard to find," McPhee told the Associated Press after Semin signed his most recent contract.

Whether Semin will remain with his Russian running mate in Washington over the long haul remains to be seen. What is certain, however, is that opposing teams will always have more difficulty trumping the Capitals when they have to worry about the heroics of two great Alexanders.

STATS:

	GP	G	A	Pts	PIM
RS	392	176	178	354	394
PO	37	12	18	30	36

DEFENSEMEN
LEGENDS

Raymond Bourque............................100
Chris Chelios..................................102
King Clancy....................................104
Dit Clapper 106
Paul Coffey....................................108
Doug Harvey 110
Tim Horton 112
Red Kelly.......................................114
Nicklas Lidstrom..............................116
Bobby Orr 118
Brad Park 120
Pierre Pilote...................................122
Denis Potvin...................................124
Larry Robinson................................126
Eddie Shore 128

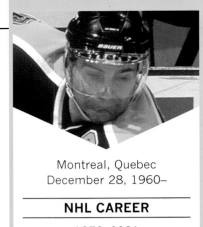

RAYMOND BOURQUE

Montreal, Quebec
December 28, 1960–

NHL CAREER

1979–2001
Boston, Colorado

On October 11, 1979 — just before his first NHL game — Raymond Bourque was handed sweater No. 7. He was naive enough not to fathom the implications of donning Phil Esposito's old number; fortunately for Bourque, his success was immediate, and he didn't have to suffer the heckling most rookies wearing a legend's number would have faced. Bourque was awarded the Calder Trophy and earned First All-Star Team status that season. No. 7 seemed to suit him just fine.

It wasn't really an issue for anyone until 1987, when the Bruins decided to honor Esposito by retiring his number, although the club said that Bourque could continue to wear what had become "his" number. Bourque had great respect for all that Esposito had done for the Bruins, so a secret plan was hatched. On "Phil Esposito Night," in front of a sellout crowd in the intimate Boston Garden, Bourque stripped off his No. 7 jersey and handed it to Esposito. The retired star was visibly moved when Bourque then turned and showed the crowd his new number, 77. Bourque used 77 for the rest of his career.

Bourque was virtually a fixture at the NHL All-Star Game throughout his career. But the 1996 All-Star Game, held in Boston, stands up as a career highlight. With only 37 seconds remaining in the third period, Bourque snared the puck and rifled in the winning goal. The hometown crowd erupted with joy, much more for the goal-scorer than the victory. The lengthy ovation was renewed when Bourque was named the game's most valuable player. The other players seemed almost as pleased as Bourque himself.

Bourque's official All-Star selection at the end of his rookie year was the first of a record 17 consecutive nominations. His five Norris Trophies ranked behind only Doug Harvey and Bobby Orr. He was also runner-up to the league's best defenseman six times, including in 2000–01, when he was 40 years old. He finished his career holding numerous NHL scoring records: most career points by a defenseman (1,579), most career goals by a defenseman (410), most career assists by a defenseman (1,169), most years in the playoffs (21) and most career playoff assists by a defenseman (139). Part of the secret to

AWARDS: 1st All-Star (13), 2nd All-Star (6), Calder, Clancy, Norris (5), Stanley Cup, HHOF 2004

STATS:

	GP	G	A	Pts	PIM
RS	1,612	410	1,169	1,579	1,141
PO	214	41	139	180	171

Bourque's success was that he took nothing for granted, even after clinching a future spot in the Hockey Hall of Fame. "I love playing the game," he explained. "That's why I'm doing well. I'm still looking at it like a little kid. Every day, you've got to prove yourself, and that's how I've played this game my whole career."

Bourque went to the Stanley Cup final twice with Boston and both times led all defensemen in playoff scoring. Unfortunately the Bruins fell easily to the Edmonton Oilers on each occasion. "A Stanley Cup," said Bourque, "would be unbelievable," but he seemed fated to join a small number of illustrious players who never saw their names engraved on the Cup. After years of denying an interest in playing anywhere else, Bourque finally requested a trade to a contender after almost 21 seasons as a Bruin. He was dealt to Colorado in March 2000.

His first playoffs with the Avalanche were disappointing, but his new team dedicated their 2000–01 campaign to getting Bourque a ring. They accomplished their mission, and captain Joe Sakic gave a tearful Bourque the privilege of being the first on the team to hoist the Cup. Bourque announced his retirement the following summer. The Avalanche lifted his No. 77 to the rafters the following season, as did the Bruins. Fittingly, Phil Esposito was on hand in Boston to hand Bourque his retired sweater.

Chicago, Illinois
January 25, 1962–

NHL CAREER

1983–2004, 2005–10
Montreal, Chicago,
Detroit, Atlanta

CHRIS CHELIOS

After emigrating from Greece to the United States in 1951, Gus Chelios developed a passion for hockey and his hometown Chicago Black Hawks that he passed on to his children. "It's that pit-bull upbringing," his son Chris once joked. "They grow 'em tough in those small European countries, and I've got this temper that gets me into trouble now and then." But Chris Chelios also managed to channel some of that ferocity into stardom in the NHL.

Chelios spent two seasons at the University of Wisconsin and a year with the American national team. After he played at the 1984 Olympic Games, the Montreal Canadiens were ready for him. He played the remainder of the 1983–84 campaign and six more seasons in Montreal, highlighted by a Stanley Cup championship in 1986. "Those were great years," he recalled. "I listened and learned a lot. Playing for the Canadiens is like getting a Harvard law degree. Montreal players know what it's like to win." Chelios was awarded the Norris Trophy as the NHL's finest defenseman in 1989, 1993 and 1996.

Chelios grew as a player, but his penalty minutes also increased. "I was a real pain in my first 8 or 10 years in the league," he has confessed. "I liked going out there and being the guy people hate to play against. I thought I was more effective being mean and getting at their top players." Yet all too often, Chelios took a bad penalty. After the Canadiens made a quick exit in the 1990 playoffs, Chelios was traded to the Blackhawks for the flashy little centerman Denis Savard.

Savard had been a crowd favorite in the Windy City, and the trade for Chelios was initially an unpopular move. But Chelios quickly endeared himself to the Chicago fans. He played a nasty game, accumulating career-high penalty time in his first three seasons as a Blackhawk, with 192, 245 and 282 minutes, respectively.

"I'm going to have to find a line between being mean and taking penalties," Chelios remarked after serving a suspension in 1994, and he was somewhat successful. "I'm trying to control myself more now," he said. "I don't want to be known as the type of player who is constantly in trouble. I want to show I can play aggressively and be mean but not jeopardize the team's success." Team success with Chicago was fleeting at best, although Chelios' play remained stellar.

"He was hard-working and down to earth in high school, and he's still like that today," said Frank Kiszka in 1998, the hockey moderator at Mount Carmel High School, where Chelios played for two years. "He's still very much 'South Side.'"

AWARDS: 1st All-Star (6), 2nd All-Star (2),
Norris (3), Stanley Cup (3)

STATS:

	GP	G	A	Pts	PIM
RS	1,651	185	763	948	2,891
PO	266	31	113	144	423

Rather than test the free-agent waters in 1997, Chelios signed a contract extension committing him to Chicago until age 38, for a salary less than market value — a move that struck many as a breath of fresh air. "Money doesn't motivate me," claimed Chelios. "I play hockey because I love it, and I was fortunate enough to go back home and have my whole family together again…. To me, it's a great honor to play in the NHL, and especially for the Blackhawks."

Sadly, Chelios' loyalty wasn't reciprocated; Chicago traded him to Detroit in March 1999. Chelios flourished as a Red Wing. After missing most of the previous campaign due to a knee injury, in 2001–02 he was voted to the First All-Star Team (his seventh All-Star berth), was runner-up for the Norris Trophy and earned his second Stanley Cup ring.

Chelios was the oldest player in the NHL in the 2007–08 season (he turned 46 mid-season; only Gordie Howe played in the NHL at an older age), and although he played a lesser role in the Red Wings' Cup win he still had an itch to play the game. When he couldn't crack the Detroit lineup midway through the following season, he headed to the farm team in the American Hockey League, and he then signed with the AHL's Chicago Wolves for the 2008–09 season. His steady play and leadership skills prompted the Atlanta Thrashers to sign him to a two-way contract mid-season, and he played seven more NHL games in the Thrashers' unsuccessful late-season charge for a playoff berth. He returned to the Wolves to finish the season and then retired. Now working in Detroit's front office, Chelios is truly a champion for the ages.

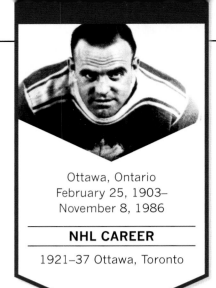

KING CLANCY

At first, Frank Clancy's nickname was an inside joke. His father, an Ottawa sports celebrity with a reputation for toughness, had earned the royal designation "King of the Heelers" in the 1890s for his ability to "heel" the ball out of a football scrum. Only an 18-year-old, 127-pound sprite when he first approached the Ottawa Senators in 1921, the junior "King" earned a spot on the defending Stanley Cup–champion Ottawa roster because of his spirit and fleetness. Signed as a substitute player, Clancy saw little ice time for a couple of years, except in practice.

"They wanted me on their team, and the only opening was on defense," said Clancy. "I had to take it or leave it, and I took it." He didn't get his first real chance until the 1923 Stanley Cup final against the Western Canada Hockey League–champion Edmonton Eskimos. In the final game of a two-game, total-goals playoff, injuries knocked out two defensemen, and Clancy substituted admirably. Then he spelled Hockey Hall of Fame center Frank Nighbor and both wingers in turn. In those days, no substitution was allowed for a penalized goalie, so when Ottawa goaltender Clint Benedict took a penalty, Clancy went between the pipes. He didn't allow a goal and even raced up the ice with Benedict's big goalie stick for a shot on net. Ottawa won the

Cup, and Clancy was hailed as the team's hero.

Clancy became a regular in 1923–24. In 1927, he helped Ottawa win another Stanley Cup, and in the 1929–30 season he led all NHL defensemen in scoring, with a career-high 17 goals and 23 assists, before being traded to the Toronto Maple Leafs for the then-exorbitant sum of $35,000 and two players. Toronto owner Conn Smythe was looking for someone to fill the building he planned to construct for the start of the 1931–32 season, and Clancy didn't disappoint him. He led the Maple Leafs to their first Stanley Cup victory in the spring of 1932 — in the new Maple Leaf Gardens before capacity crowds.

Clancy earned All-Star honors in his first four seasons with Toronto, but he combined his hockey prowess with clownlike theatrics. He once provoked Boston's notorious Eddie Shore into dropping his gloves then shook Shore's hand enthusiastically while grinning and said, "Good evening, Eddie. How are you tonight?" Everyone,

AWARDS: 1st All-Star (2), 2nd All-Star (2), Stanley Cup (3), HHOF 1958

STATS:

	GP	G	A	Pts	PIM
RS	592	136	147	283	914
PO	55	8	8	16	88

including Shore, was left laughing. Although Clancy engaged in plenty of fights over the years, he didn't make many lasting enemies. The Maple Leafs decided to honor Clancy on St. Patrick's Day 1934, and the ceremony culminated in the presentation of the guest of honor dressed as Old King Cole. When the lights were momentarily extinguished, Clancy doffed a big white beard, regal robes and a crown to reveal himself garbed in a brilliant emerald-green uniform. He remained decked out in green when the game began, but the visiting New York Rangers gave Clancy such a rough time that he donned his Maple Leafs' blue-and-white for the second and third periods.

After playing only six games for Toronto in the 1936–37 season, Clancy hung up his skates — briefly. He coached the Montreal Maroons for half a season before NHL president Frank Calder asked him to switch to refereeing. "I suppose Mr. Calder figured out I knew a lot about the rule book," Clancy said, "after having spent so much time sitting and thinking in the penalty box."

Clancy retained his sense of humor in his new position of authority, and he was tolerant. "If at all possible, I avoided giving misconduct penalties," he said. "If a youngster blew his top, I quietly told him to keep cool or he would hurt his team. If an older player became abusive, I found that it helped to give him a second chance. So I would look tough and say, 'Just repeat what you said.' Usually, [the player] took the warning and skated away."

Clancy coached the Maple Leafs in the mid-1950s and again in 1972, but he served the Maple Leafs best as an unofficial goodwill ambassador, until his death in 1986. The NHL established the King Clancy Memorial Trophy in 1988, which is awarded annually to the player who best exemplifies leadership both on and off the ice while making a significant humanitarian contribution to his community.

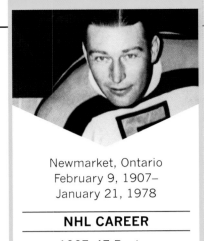

Newmarket, Ontario
February 9, 1907–
January 21, 1978

NHL CAREER

1927–47 Boston

DIT CLAPPER

Dit Clapper unintentionally coined his own nickname. Called "Vic" by his parents, as a toddler could only say "Dit," and soon that's how everyone knew him. Playing all his games for the Boston Bruins, Clapper became hockey's first 20-year man, setting the NHL longevity record. Coincidentally, Clapper's last season was Gordie Howe's first.

After Howe had established himself in the league, he admitted to one ambition — to play for 20 years, "just like Clapper." While he eventually lasted even longer than Boston's wonder, Howe was unable to challenge Clapper's other distinction in the history books: A right winger for his first 11 years in the league, Clapper hit even greater heights on the blueline. He remains the only NHL player to be awarded All-Star status both as a forward and as a defenseman.

Clapper joined Boston in 1927 at the age of 19. In his first two campaigns, he scored only four and nine goals, respectively, but the Bruins won the Stanley Cup in 1929. The following season was different: Clapper erupted with 41 goals and 20 assists in what was only a 44-game season, good for third in the NHL scoring race. His performance was well deserving of an All-Star berth, but the NHL didn't begin honoring its elite in that manner until the 1930–31 season, when Clapper was the NHL's Second All-Star Team's right winger. He was named team captain for Boston in 1932–33.

At 6-foot-2 and 200 pounds, Clapper had a size advantage over most NHL players and the strength to match. No pacifist, he nonetheless didn't play the Boston-style roughhouse as defined by bruising defensemen Lionel Hitchman and Eddie Shore. He was even known to break up fights on occasion; although once he reached his boiling point, he was capable of inflicting heavy damage with his fists. One such punch almost got him into severe trouble.

Avenging a butt-end administered to a Boston rookie in the 1936 playoffs, Clapper was punching the offending Montreal Maroons player when the referee yanked him back by the hair. That was the referee's first mistake, for Clapper took great pride in his meticulously combed jet-black hair with the razor-sharp part. The young official then further enraged

AWARDS: 1st All-Star (3), 2nd All-Star (3), Stanley Cup (3), HHOF 1947

STATS:

	GP	G	A	Pts	PIM
RS	833	228	246	474	462
PO	82	13	17	30	50

Clapper by denigrating his mother. Stunned by the comment, Clapper asked the referee to repeat himself. When he did, Clapper decked him.

The referee was Clarence Campbell, who 10 years later would become president of the NHL. Knowing Clapper's character and recognizing the role he himself had played, Campbell made a public apology and explained the circumstances to league president Frank Calder. Instead of receiving a lengthy suspension, Clapper was fined $100.

After 11 years at right wing, Clapper moved back to defense. At the end of the 1938–39 season, Clapper joined Shore as a First All-Star Team defensemen. The two rearguards were also an important part of Boston's Stanley Cup victory that spring. Clapper made the First All-Star Team the next two seasons as well.

Boston's 1940–41 team emerged as one of the strongest in NHL history. Clapper was runner-up in Hart Trophy voting to teammate Bill Cowley, and the Bruins swept Detroit in the Stanley Cup final. Clapper then earned a Second All-Star Team spot in 1943–44. In addition to retaining him as captain, Boston's general manager Art Ross relinquished his coaching responsibilities and appointed Clapper player/coach for the 1945–46 campaign.

Clapper filled the role for a little more than two years before hanging up his skates and moving into coaching full-time. After almost three seasons behind the bench, though, Clapper had had enough. "Being a coach is a lousy job," he said in a surprise resignation speech on April 1, 1949. "I couldn't abuse these players. They're my friends."

Clapper was inducted into the Hockey Hall of Fame the day after he retired from active play, and his No. 5 jersey was raised to the rafters of the Boston Garden almost as quickly. Having reached hockey's pinnacles, Clapper severed his ties with the professional game, moved back to Canada and opened a sporting-goods store.

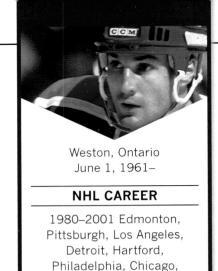

Weston, Ontario
June 1, 1961–

NHL CAREER

1980–2001 Edmonton,
Pittsburgh, Los Angeles,
Detroit, Hartford,
Philadelphia, Chicago,
Carolina, Boston

PAUL COFFEY

When Paul Coffey emerged as an offensive star in the early 1980s, he drew inevitable comparisons to superstar Bobby Orr. However, he bore that heavy burden of expectation successfully.

Frank Mahovlich made a huge impression on Coffey's father, and as a boy, Paul was coaxed to emulate "The Big M" and make every stride as long and strong as possible. "I would never have become a hockey player," he once admitted, "but for my father." Coffey's fluid and graceful style led many to remark that he could glide faster than most players could skate.

Playing for Glen Sather on the Edmonton Oilers added a further dimension to his game. Sather noted his rookie's speed and encouraged Coffey to jump up into the play more often. "I'd never done that before," said Coffey, "even in junior." The results were dramatic. As the fourth man in the rush, Coffey was a key to the Oilers' offense; not only did he skate fast, he was also capable of making a sterling setup or finishing a play with his accurate shot.

After a decent rookie year, with nine goals and 23 assists, Coffey almost tripled his offensive production with an 89-point sophomore season, in 1981–82, and made either the First or Second All-Star Team for each of the next five seasons. His point totals continued to climb as he helped

the franchise win its first two Stanley Cups, in 1984 and 1985. His stellar play, which included 12 goals and 25 assists in the 1985 playoffs, led many to believe that he should have won the Conn Smythe Trophy that year, but Wayne Gretzky, who had amassed 10 more points, won the award. Coffey peaked offensively with a record-breaking 48-goal, 90-assist campaign in 1985–86 and won his second consecutive Norris Trophy, but the Oilers were eliminated in the second round of the playoffs. The team rebounded to win the Cup again the next year, but in the midst of the celebrations Coffey dropped a bombshell: His days as an Edmonton Oiler were over.

Coffey sought to renegotiate his contract but felt denigrated by Edmonton owner Peter Pocklington. He was adamant that he wouldn't play for "Peter Puck" again. He was traded to the Pittsburgh Penguins in 1987. Mario Lemieux was the perfect receiver for the long-bomb passes for

AWARDS: 1st All-Star (4), 2nd All-Star (4), Norris (3), Stanley Cup (4), HHOF 2004

STATS:

	GP	G	A	Pts	PIM
RS	1,409	396	1,135	1,531	1,802
PO	194	59	137	196	264

which Coffey was famous. In 1991, Lemieux got the Stanley Cup ring he coveted, and Coffey earned his fourth. However, while the Penguins were en route to their second consecutive Cup, Coffey was traded to the Los Angeles Kings.

"Hockey's a funny game," Coffey observed. "You have to prove yourself every shift, every game." Despite all that he had done, Coffey hadn't always received his due.

In his 1988 autobiography, Larry Robinson had high regard for Coffey: "Coffey has the uncanny ability to make a defensive play in his own end and start the puck back the other way before the other team can react," and he opined that Coffey was "probably the best player in hockey today when it comes to the transition game."

Dealt to Detroit in January 1993, Coffey won his third Norris Trophy in 1995 as a Red Wing. The remainder of his career was less successful. Unhappy with his 1996 trade to Hartford, Coffey was dealt to Philadelphia after 20 games with the hapless Whalers. After two seasons with the Flyers, he made brief stays in Chicago, Carolina and Boston before retiring in the summer of 2001.

When Coffey hung up his skates, his 1,135 career assists and 1,531 points placed him fourth and ninth, respectively, in the NHL record books. He was inducted into the Hockey Hall of Fame in 2004, and in 2005 Edmonton retired his No. 7.

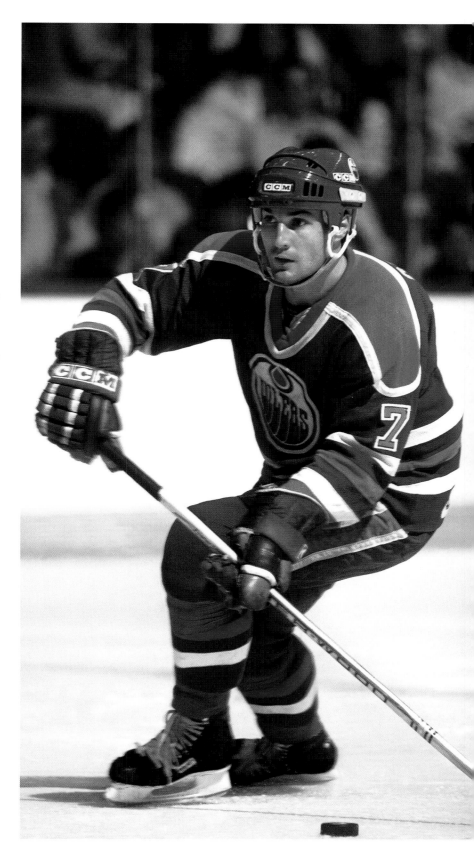

Montreal, Quebec
December 19, 1924–
December 26, 1989

NHL CAREER

1947–64, 1966–69
Montreal, NY Rangers,
Detroit, St. Louis

DOUG HARVEY

Few kings have fallen further from grace than Doug Harvey, who died in 1989 at the age of 65 in a Montreal hospital after living for several impoverished years on the fringes of society. At his peak, Harvey ruled the NHL blueline for more than a dozen years, winning the Norris Trophy as the league's best defenseman seven out of eight seasons between 1955 and 1962. Diagnosed late in life with manic-depressive disorder, his death from cirrhosis was the predictable result of years of using alcohol to deal with his wild mood swings. Although he had quit drinking three years before his death, the damage to his liver was irreversible.

Harvey was one of the smartest players ever to lace on skates, but he wasn't always appreciated. His deliberate and efficient manner initially struck many as lackadaisical. Instead of racing up and down the ice, Harvey moved methodically, breaking up opposition rushes with an economical poke-check or coolly intercepting a pass when it looked as though he was out of position. He'd keep the puck on his stick while almost motionless, and then, just before the opposition stripped him of it, he'd flick a beautiful pass. Nor was Harvey averse to carrying the puck in front of his own net. Such hockey heresy gave management fits until they realized his apparently reckless and lazy maneuvers were actually planned and executed almost perfectly.

Harvey had the ability to dictate play. Often referred to as the team's "quarterback," he could slow a game's pace by corralling the puck and shepherding his team up the ice, or he could ignite the action by snapping long lead passes to a fleet of sharpshooters. The combination was so deadly on the power play — with Montreal exploding with two or three goals in a two-minute span — that the league changed the rules in 1956 to allow a penalized player back on the ice as soon as his team was scored upon.

Harvey was such an integral part of Montreal's dynasty in the 1950s that in 1957, when he teamed up with Detroit's Ted Lindsay in a failed attempt to form a Players' Association, the Canadiens refused to "exile" their star defenseman to the lowly Chicago Black Hawks, as some clubs had done to other association

AWARDS: 1st All-Star (10), 2nd All-Star, Norris (7), Stanley Cup (6), HHOF 1973

STATS:

	GP	G	A	Pts	PIM
RS	1,113	88	452	540	1,216
PO	137	8	64	72	152

supporters. Harvey was a leader both on the ice and in the dressing room, where his sense of humor and lighthearted approach made him the life of every party. While this endeared him to his teammates, Montreal management eventually decided that he was more trouble than he was worth and traded him in 1961.

In 1961–62, Harvey joined the New York Rangers as player/coach, and, even with his additional responsibilities, he won his seventh Norris Trophy and got the sad-sack Rangers into the playoffs. Missing being "one of the boys," however, Harvey relinquished his coaching duties the following season.

Harvey continued to play, but though his mental skills were still sharp, his age and lifestyle were starting to catch up with him. Early in the 1963–64 season, the Rangers demoted him to the minors, where he bounced around for five years with a number of teams. He returned to the NHL in 1967, after the expansion, and he joined the St. Louis Blues for the 1967–68 playoffs, chipping in four assists, and played for them the following season, at the age of 44. He then scouted professionally but, before long, had worked himself out of hockey altogether, gathering notice for only a few days when news of his illness and subsequent death was broadcast.

Cochrane, Ontario
January 12, 1930–
February 21, 1974

NHL CAREER

1949–74 Toronto,
NY Rangers, Pittsburgh,
Buffalo

TIM HORTON

Tim Horton's name lives on through the chain of coffee and donut shops he founded, but regrettably few patrons remember the outstanding hockey player who launched the business. Horton was recognized as an NHL All-Star six times and was runner-up in Norris Trophy voting twice, the second time when he was 39 years old. Generally acknowledged as the strongest man in the game while he was playing, Horton skated through most of 24 NHL seasons. "There were defensemen you had to fear because they were vicious and would slam you into the boards from behind," declared Bobby Hull, perhaps the only player in the league more muscular than Horton. "But you respected Horton because he didn't need that type of intimidation. He used his tremendous strength and talent to keep you in check."

"If he'd only get angry," King Clancy once lamented, "no one would top him in this league." However, Horton believed he had taken too many penalties early in his career because of his "hot temper."

Rather than punching back at an angry opponent, he'd envelop his foe in a crushing bear hug. Derek Sanderson once bit Horton during a fight; years later, Horton's widow, Lori, asked him why. "Well," Sanderson replied, "I felt one

rib go, and I felt another rib go, so I just had to get out of there!" Horton accumulated 518 points over his lengthy career, a huge total in his day. Even though he reportedly measured a couple of inches less than his official 5-foot-10, Horton was a menacing sight as he crossed the opposition blueline with his almost fully erect skating style and the momentum of a freight train.

In 1955 defenseman Bill Gadsby caught Horton on a rare occasion when his head was down with "the hardest check in my life." Horton suffered a broken leg and jaw, the worst of a litany of injuries suffered over the years. Horton's daughters begged him to let his crew cut grow longer in the 1970s, not so much to keep up with the day's fashion but to hide his numerous scars. Yet injuries and age seemed to be little more than minor inconveniences to Horton.

His "retirement" was an almost routine event at contract-renewal time, but when the Maple Leafs fired Punch Imlach, who liked to prolong and resurrect older players' careers, the 39-year-old Horton declared, "If this team doesn't want Imlach, I guess it doesn't want me."

Toronto owner Harold Ballard asked Horton later in the summer of 1969 whether he'd consider playing again for more money. "If somebody said they'd double my salary," Horton

joked, "I might consider it." Ballard took him up on his jest, and Horton went from $45,000 to $90,000 a season. However, the Maple Leafs dealt Horton to the New York Rangers late in the 1969–70 campaign.

Horton retired after his second year with the Rangers, but his old teammate Red Kelly convinced him to play a year for him in Pittsburgh. Although Horton's partner wanted him to focus on the donut business, Imlach talked Horton into joining his new club, the Buffalo Sabres, in 1972. "Maybe it's just a bad habit I've acquired," Horton joked. "I like to play hockey. I have a long time ahead of me to sit behind a desk."

In negotiating what proved to be Horton's final contract, Imlach, to his lasting regret, gave Horton the car of his choice as part of his compensation. A lifelong automobile enthusiast, Horton chose a Ford Pantera — a sports car capable of dangerously high speeds. Horton was killed instantly in a single-vehicle accident in 1974 while returning home to Buffalo from a game where, fittingly, he had been named third star in Maple Leaf Gardens.

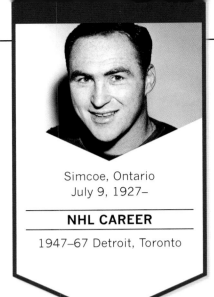

Simcoe, Ontario
July 9, 1927–

NHL CAREER

1947–67 Detroit, Toronto

RED KELLY

Red Kelly was the last defenseman to win the Lady Byng Trophy. In the early 1950s, he made the award almost a personal possession by winning it three out of four years and coming second in the other. "Kelly is as good a player as I've seen in my long connection with hockey, which dates back to 1906," said Montreal general manager Frank Selke Sr. in 1952. "More than that, he exemplifies everything that is desirable in a young man, and the Detroit club is fortunate to have a man of his integrity and character in its lineup."

Kelly was tough — he won a welterweight boxing championship during his junior days at St. Mike's in Toronto. Looking back at his hockey career, Kelly recalled: "I had some good fights with some tough players. But I also knew that fighting hurts the hands and takes you off the ice."

Fleet of foot and creative with the puck, Kelly was a league All-Star for eight consecutive seasons. Some maintain the Norris Trophy was created specifically to honor him, and he was its first recipient as the league's best defenseman in the 1953–54 season. Yet the red-haired defender remained an offensive threat; he led NHL defensemen in goals eight times. His role in Detroit's four Stanley Cup wins in the 1950s is often forgotten, but Kelly was a critical component of a powerhouse club. He played up to 55 minutes a game, leading many to believe he would quickly burn out, but he was indefatigable and lasted 20 years in the NHL.

Early in 1960, Kelly was prodded into revealing to the media that the Red Wings had coaxed him into playing on a broken ankle during the previous season. General manager Jack Adams immediately traded him to the New York Rangers. Kelly refused to report and began a life outside the game. An exploratory call from King Clancy and the Toronto Maple Leafs 10 days later proved fruitful, and a new deal was swung. However, the Maple Leafs weren't looking for a defenseman.

"One year, Sid Abel got hurt in the playoffs," said Kelly, "and they moved me to center between Howe and Lindsay. I believe I also lost a First All-Star selection one year because of helping out on the forward line. The voters didn't know where to put me." With Kelly as his centerman in 1960–61, Frank Mahovlich finally

AWARDS: 1st All-Star (6), 2nd All-Star (2), Byng (4), Norris, Stanley Cup (8), HHOF 1969

STATS:

	GP	G	A	Pts	PIM
RS	1,316	281	542	823	327
PO	164	33	59	92	51

realized his potential, netting 48 goals. Kelly had his first 20-goal season and 50 helpers, with a paltry 12 minutes in penalties, to earn his fourth and final Lady Byng Trophy.

While center Kelly helped the Maple Leafs win the Stanley Cup four out of the next six years, he also served as a member of Parliament for his Toronto riding, commuting to Ottawa for four seasons. He was elected twice but finally gave up his second job to focus on the game. "I thought that the greatest stickhandlers were in hockey," he said after retiring from elected office, "but I found out they were in Parliament."

After hoisting the Stanley Cup in his last season, the 40-year-old Kelly retired from active play as the record-holder for most career playoff games, at 164. He began his career as a coach with the Los Angeles Kings in 1967–68 for their inaugural season. Two years later, he joined the Pittsburgh Penguins for several seasons before returning to Toronto to coach.

Kelly guided the Maple Leafs for four complete seasons, and he is fondly remembered in Toronto for his introduction of "Pyramid Power," a positive-thinking campaign. Kelly had pyramids under the bench and in the dressing room and provided smaller ones for his players to sleep with. The

novelty eventually wore off — Toronto lost to Philadelphia in the quarterfinals for three successive years — and Kelly retired from the game after the 1976–77 season.

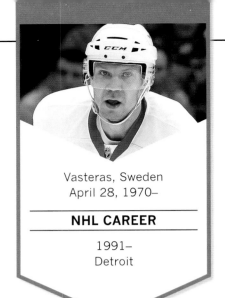

Vasteras, Sweden
April 28, 1970–

NHL CAREER

1991–
Detroit

NICKLAS LIDSTROM

Nicklas Lidstrom scored his first career hat trick on December 15, 2010. "He's done everything else," noted Detroit Red Wings coach Mike Babcock. "He might as well do that." With great skill and consistency, Lidstrom has established himself as the dominant defenseman of his era.

At the launch of his career, he had the thrill of playing with Borje Salming, his childhood idol, in the 1991 Canada Cup tournament. Lidstrom has gone on to not only eclipse Salming as the greatest Swedish defenseman to lace up skates, but arguably to rank as the best European to ever play in the National Hockey League. Lidstrom joined the Red Wings right after that Canada Cup tourney and finished runner-up to the "Russian Rocket" Pavel Bure for 1991–92 Rookie of the Year honors. Yet his transition to the North American game wasn't easy.

"You aren't used to yelling in English on the ice," he recalled, "So at first, you are just reacting. You are thinking in Swedish and slowly translating into English. I had to simplify my game. I had to play safe, minimize mistakes and get rid of the puck a lot quicker."

Lidstrom tallied an impressive 11 goals and 49 assists as a rookie, and offense has been one of the hallmarks of his career. He has averaged more than 50 points a season, setting all the noteworthy defensemen scoring records in Detroit.

Not an overtly physical player, Lidstrom uses finesse and savvy rather than power. He is the first defenseman since Red Kelly, in the 1950s, to get serious consideration for the Lady Byng Trophy for gentlemanly play, and he's averaged less than 30 penalty minutes per season. "I always try to be in the right position," he explained, "Because I'm not going to go out and put the big hit on someone. That's just not my game."

"He makes the right move just about all the time," noted long-time Detroit coach Scotty Bowman, praising Lidstrom's efficiency in separating the opposition from the puck. "He plays in control, and his stick is almost always in the right position."

Bowman also praised Lidstrom's ability to be an offensive threat while rarely getting caught up ice, citing "The best player I ever coached" as having a "sixth sense" in knowing what is going on all over the ice.

After three straight seasons finishing runner-up for the Norris Trophy, Lidstrom was finally named the NHL's top blueliner in 2001. He has been nominated just about every year since and has won the Norris seven times now. Only Bobby Orr with eight wins, has won it more.

Yet Lidstrom's lengthy NHL career, all in

Detroit, almost came to a premature end. Just after the Red Wings broke a 42-year drought and won the Stanley Cup in the spring of 1997, as his oldest children neared school age during the 1997–98 campaign and Lidstrom seriously considered returning to Sweden in order to give his family a more rooted upbringing and have them educated in their native tongue. "My family comes first," he stated firmly. "I've always said that. When I first came over, I thought I might stay two or three years," he explained. "I just wanted to see if I could play at this level." Lidstrom mulled over his options for most of the season, finally settling on remaining with Detroit.

Lidstrom helped the Red Wings defend their crown in the spring of 1998, and Detroit won again in 2001–02, when Lidstrom was awarded the Conn Smythe Trophy — the first European to be named most valuable player in the playoffs. An alternate captain since the 1997–98 season, Lidstrom assumed the Detroit "C" when the legendary Steve Yzerman retired in 2006. Less than two years later, Lidstrom had the captain's honor of being the first to lift the Cup when the Red Wings prevailed in the spring of 2008, the fourth championship of his career.

Lidstrom has the rare distinction of having won a gold medal in the World Championship (1991) and the Olympics (2006) in addition to his Stanley Cup rings. A 12-time NHL All-Star (10 on the First Team), his career milestones are setting longevity records for both a European player in the NHL and a Detroit defenseman. He remains a serious competitor for personal NHL awards and a spot in the Hockey Hall of Fame no doubt awaits him.

AWARDS: 1st All-Star (10), 2nd All-Star (2), Norris (7), Smythe, Stanley Cup (4)

STATS:

	GP	G	A	Pts	PIM
RS	1,494	253	855	1,108	486
PO	258	54	129	183	76

Parry Sound, Ontario
March 20, 1948–

NHL CAREER

1966–79 Boston, Chicago

BOBBY ORR

Doug Orr was one of the speediest hockey players ever seen in Parry Sound, Ontario, and he had a young son with tremendous potential. He thought his boy Bobby should play forward; after all, Bobby was fast on his skates, could stickhandle like the devil and had both a hard shot and a deft scoring touch.

Fortunately for hockey, Bucko McDonald — a standout NHL defenseman in the 1930s and 1940s — was head coach of all the Parry Sound boys' teams and felt Bobby should play defense, maintaining that he was a natural at the position. "Bucko taught me almost everything I know," Orr later declared graciously.

"It wasn't hard," McDonald confessed, "because even at that age, you could see that Bobby was special." The little defenseman soon came to the attention of the Boston Bruins, who did everything they could to ensure Orr became, and remained, their exclusive property.

In deference to Orr's youth, Boston made exceptional arrangements to allow him to play for the Oshawa Generals, who played in Ontario's best junior league, in 1962. The 14-year-old Orr continued to live at home, 150 miles from Oshawa, and was driven to every game. He didn't practice with the team once, yet at the end of the season he was selected to the Second All-Star Team.

Orr dominated junior hockey for three more years. When he finally made his Boston debut in 1966, the hockey prodigy lived up to his advance billing — and more.

Orr's 13 goals and 41 points in his first NHL campaign may seem humble, but only Chicago's Pierre Pilote tallied more as a defenseman that season. Orr earned the Calder Trophy as the NHL's outstanding rookie and a Second All-Star Team selection.

While most teams had included at least one rushing defenseman since Eddie Shore's day, Orr took the concept to another level. His radical approach to the game invited argument, including the one Bucko McDonald had won years earlier. "We played him at center for six or seven games in his rookie year," said Harry Sinden, Orr's first coach in Boston. "He was only tremendous. On defense, he was phenomenal."

AWARDS: 1st All-Star (8), 2nd All-Star, Calder, Hart (3), Norris (8), Pearson, Ross (2), Smythe (2), Stanley Cup (2), HHOF 1979

STATS:

	GP	G	A	Pts	PIM
RS	657	270	645	915	953
PO	74	26	66	92	107

Orr went on to set offensive records, twice winning the Art Ross Trophy as the NHL's leading scorer and finishing as runner-up for the award to teammate Phil Esposito three times. In 1970–71, Orr set the high mark for assists and total points by a defenseman with 37 goals and 102 assists, a record that still stands.

Orr won the Norris Trophy for eight consecutive years. He blocked shots, cleared the front of his net and dropped his gloves when the situation called for it. But his lasting legacy is the way he spearheaded the attack. "One of his great gifts," noted the analytical Eddie Shore, "is the ability to gauge precisely the speed of the man he is passing to."

Orr's 1970 goal to win Boston's first Stanley Cup in 29 years is remembered best — his hands raised in celebration as he is hoisted in the air by St. Louis defenseman Noel Picard. Derek Sanderson, who fed him the puck that day, commented: "We had the one player who could finish a play like that."

"Winning the Cup twice was great," Orr told *The Hockey News*, "but I wonder why we didn't win it more often." Due in part to his being betrayed by his now-disgraced agent Alan Eagleson, Orr regretfully forsook Boston to sign a free-agent contract with the Chicago Black Hawks in June 1976. But his greatest disappointment was his forced early retirement. Plagued by knee injuries throughout his career (he even sat out all of the 1977–78 season to recover), Orr was finished at the age of 30. He played fewer than 10 seasons, but he left an indelible mark on the game. "Losing Bobby," said Gordie Howe, "was the biggest blow the NHL has ever suffered."

Toronto, Ontario
July 6, 1948–

NHL CAREER

1968–85 NY Rangers,
Boston, Detroit

BRAD PARK

When he negotiated his son's first NHL contract, Brad Park's father got a verbal agreement from New York Rangers general manager Emile Francis that Brad would be paired with defenseman Harry Howell, a 16-year NHL veteran. "I knew that I could learn a lot by watching Harry," said Brad Park, "but he really went out of his way to work with me. I learned so many little things just in the four weeks I spent in my first Rangers training camp. Most of them were mental aspects of the game — how to foresee or deal with different situations." By his second season, Park was a league All-Star, a status he held for seven of the next 10 years.

Park played a rugged, hard-hitting game and became the team's policeman. He fought a lot, yet his point totals continued to rise along with his penalty minutes. The Rangers made it to the Stanley Cup final in 1972 but lost to the Boston Bruins in a six-game battle. "Bobby Orr was the difference," said Park, who finished runner-up to Orr in Norris Trophy voting that season for the third time in a row.

Even though Park led his team in assists (57) and points (82) in 1973–74, he lost out to Orr again. "For a while, I guess, I was trying to compete with him," Park admitted that year. The self-assured Park allowed that while he might be slightly better than his rival defensively, Orr's speed allowed him to make mistakes and still get back into position. "But let's face it," Park added, "there's only one Bobby Orr. From now on, I'm just going to be Brad Park."

Park was named team captain for the 1974–75 season, but early the following season, Rangers management deemed a shake-up necessary. Park, Jean Ratelle and Joe Zanussi were sent to archrival Boston in return for Phil Esposito and Carol Vadnais. On record as hating both Boston and Bruins fans, Park couldn't have been less pleased. There was a silver lining, though: He would be playing with Bobby Orr.

Boston coach Don Cherry decided his two blueline stars would spell each other so that one would be on the ice at all times, but he had them man power plays together. Park described their efficiency in converting the manpower advantage into goals as "about 50 percent"; unfortunately, the combination lasted for only 10 games before Orr's knees gave out.

"Don Cherry asked me to sit back and concentrate on the defensive side of the game," said Park, "unless I was on the power play or we were behind late in the game. Many wondered if I had lost a step." Cherry later speculated that his instructions cost Park a Norris Trophy — he

came second behind Denis Potvin twice — but noted that he probably helped prolong a Hockey Hall of Fame career at the same time. Although Park underwent nine operations on his left knee, he didn't miss a season or the Stanley Cup playoffs for 17 years. He went to the final twice with the Bruins, but a championship was just not in the cards for him.

A free agent in 1983, Park finished his playing career in Detroit, where he finally got his name on some NHL hardware in 1984: the Bill Masterton Trophy in recognition of his perseverance and dedication to hockey. His subsequent coaching career in Detroit was short. "I took over a last-place team," said Park, "and I kept them there." He was fired after 45 games.

Park was also deeply involved in legal action against NHL owners for salary collusion in the 1970s. The suit was eventually dismissed, when it was ruled the statute of limitations had run out.

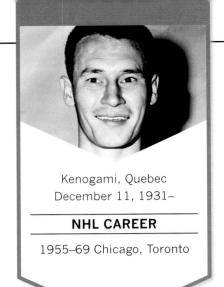

Kenogami, Quebec
December 11, 1931–

NHL CAREER

1955–69 Chicago, Toronto

PIERRE PILOTE

"My first pair of skates was my mother's," said Pierre Pilote, "and I didn't play organized hockey until I was 17." From such humble beginnings arose one of the NHL's premier defensemen. Pilote won the Norris Trophy three years in a row and sandwiched those victories with three second-place finishes. A successful rushing defenseman in the NHL's Original Six era, Pilote was honored as an All-Star for eight consecutive years, five in a row on the First Team. That Pilote's name is not as celebrated as some who accomplished less may owe as much to the nasty side of his game as it does to his team's relative lack of success. Back then, if you weren't a Chicago Black Hawks fan, you probably hated Pilote.

"When penalties came, I always made sure I got my money's worth," confessed Pilote. "The guy paid for it, whether it was from boarding or charging, and I saw that as a sign that I was in the game." A definite part of his strategy was intimidation, a technique he first honed as a teenager. After moving to Fort Erie, Ontario, from Kenogami, Quebec, he started to play industrial-league hockey. "You'd call it a butcher league now," claimed Pilote. He once joked that the first English words he learned were "Do you want to fight?"

In 1952–53, Pilote joined the Buffalo Bisons of the American Hockey League. He apprenticed for over three years under player-coach Frank Eddolls, a former NHL defenseman. "Frank taught me that the game was simple and uncomplicated, if you played it right," said Pilote. "The short pass rather than the long rink-wide kind was the key to movement, the key to the attack." Pilote got his first call-up to the Black Hawks in 1955–56, and by the next year he was there to stay.

Although only 5-foot-9 and 180 pounds, Pilote played with determination and an obvious mean streak. He pulled no punches when clearing the front of his net. Yet he had a light touch in moving the puck, either by passing or by skating it up ice, and he steadily refined every facet of his emerging skills.

By the 1959–60 season, he was the NHL's leading scorer among defensemen, with seven goals and 38 assists, and was named to the Second

AWARDS: 1st All-Star (5), 2nd All-Star (3), Norris (3), Stanley Cup, HHOF 1975

STATS:

	GP	G	A	Pts	PIM
RS	890	80	418	498	1,251
PO	86	8	53	61	102

All-Star Team. The following season, Pilote led the league with 165 penalty minutes and made a major contribution to Chicago's Stanley Cup win in the spring of 1961. He tied Gordie Howe for the most playoff points, with three goals and 12 helpers, including assists on three game-winners in the final, and the Black Hawks defeated the Red Wings to end their 23-year Cup drought — a feat not repeated for almost 50 years.

A pioneer in the use of visualization, Pilote spent hours analyzing his own play and that of his teammates and opponents and imagining possible situations on the ice. "Tommy Ivan [Chicago's general manager] once told me I could see things other players couldn't," said Pilote, but his quick reactions and uncanny anticipation came both from his mental practice and from continuous hard work. He also set high personal goals. Pilote won his first Norris Trophy in 1962–63, and the next season he recorded 46 assists, tying an NHL best. In 1964–65, he broke Babe Pratt's record of 57 points by a defenseman (set in the 1943–44 season), with 14 goals and 45 assists.

Pilote was still team captain when Chicago traded him to Toronto in the summer of 1968. His subsequent season's total of 46 penalty minutes with Toronto was a career low, a sign that

some of the edge was gone from his game. Pilote decided it was time to retire. He was elected to the Hockey Hall of Fame in 1975.

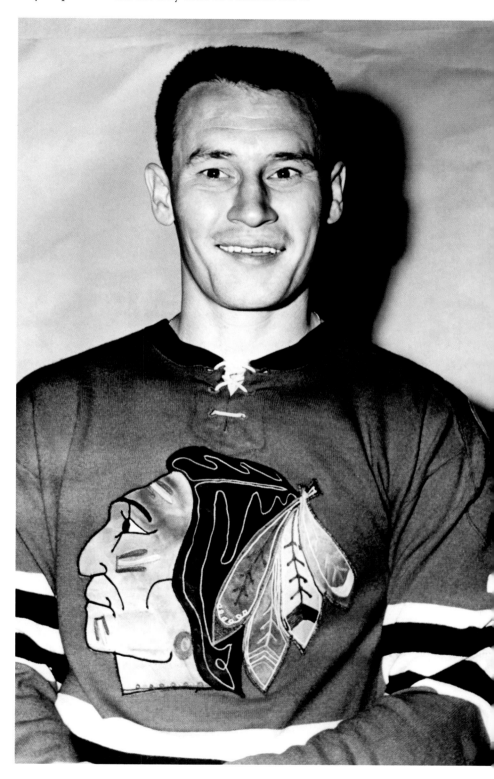

Ottawa, Ontario
October 29, 1953–

NHL CAREER

1973–88 NY Islanders

DENIS POTVIN

A precocious child, bigger and stronger than others his age, Denis Potvin had a temperament that would make him one of the most intimidating defensemen in NHL history. "I didn't want to become known as a bully," he recalled, "yet I had a fanatical obsession with being the best." At the age of 13, he joined his 17-year-old brother Jean's junior team, the Ottawa 67s, and made an immediate impression. "Potvin Touted as Next Bobby Orr" was the headline of the day and of the next decade.

Potvin first experienced the pleasures of hitting while playing football and discovered that he could have that feeling on the ice too. "I found a similar thrill going into the corners, feeling the crunch of body against body, stick against stick," he said. "In a purely impersonal sense, I enjoyed hurting people with my body, as long as they weren't seriously injured."

Leo Boivin, one of the most devastating body checkers in NHL history, coached Potvin for his last year of junior eligibility and helped him fine-tune his hip-checking technique — a dying art. But Potvin was frustrated. At the time, NHL rules strictly prohibited players under the age of 20. Nevertheless, with 123 points in 1972–73, Potvin beat Bobby Orr's record and set a new mark for junior defensemen that lasted for 16 seasons.

"Orr does things I don't do, and I do things he doesn't do," he said confidently. "You can't compare us."

The last-place New York Islanders selected Potvin as their first pick in the 1973 entry draft. "Now that I'm here," said Potvin, "I ask myself, 'What am I going to do next?' Well, I want to be the best. I set my goals high. It keeps you working; it keeps you alive." He won Rookie of the Year honors and was named the Islanders team captain in the fall of 1979.

"We know we can beat the Rangers," Potvin said when entering the 1975 playoffs against the Islanders' crosstown rivals. "We're younger, stronger, better. For some reason, though, we have too much respect for them. We treat them like gods." His team then proceeded to sweep the Rangers out of the playoffs. Potvin's first selection as First All-Star Team defenseman coincided with Orr's last.

Potvin later admitted that the confidence he displayed was a "security blanket," masking a deep-seated fear of failure. He hit the 30-goal mark late in his third season — a magic number for a defenseman, which only Orr had reached — and he almost collapsed with relief. "I skated to the bench," recalled Potvin, "fell to the wooden plank and bawled as quietly as I could before

AWARDS: 1st All-Star (5), 2nd All-Star (2), Calder, Norris (3), Stanley Cup (4), HHOF 1991

STATS:

	GP	G	A	Pts	PIM
RS	1,060	310	742	1,052	1,356
PO	185	56	108	164	253

14,865 friends." He won the Norris Trophy that same season, ending Orr's eight-year monopoly.

In the 1976 Canada Cup tournament that fall, Potvin led the international meet in points and in the plus/minus category, but Orr received the award as most valuable player. "Is Bobby Orr only going to have to play to be known as the best defenseman?" he fumed in a candid diary he kept for a Canadian magazine. But he gradually received more of the respect he craved.

"Potvin could hurt you in so many ways," said Islanders coach Al Arbour, "with a defensive play or a pass or a goal from the point. He also had a mean streak, so he could hurt with his stick or just physically, with his body." While Potvin won two more Norris Trophies during the 1970s, he felt hobbled by Arbour, who had been a "defensive defenseman" for 16 NHL seasons. However, Potvin's all-around game was a key to the Islanders' four consecutive Stanley Cup wins in the 1980s.

Potvin retired on his own terms in 1988, holding the records for the most goals, assists and points by an NHL defenseman.

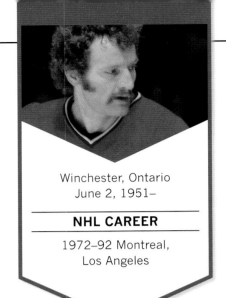

Winchester, Ontario
June 2, 1951–

NHL CAREER

1972–92 Montreal,
Los Angeles

LARRY ROBINSON

Larry Robinson's selection at the 1971 NHL entry draft was not a big story at the time. Montreal made Guy Lafleur its first prize, although general manager Sam Pollock had a pocketful of extra picks, typically hornswoggled from NHL expansion teams. Robinson was the Canadiens' fourth choice. But "Big Bird" Robinson, gangly and tough, and Lafleur "The Flower," smooth and graceful, would soon represent the careful balance of yet another Montreal dynasty. Before that day came, however, each would have to serve an apprenticeship.

Lafleur joined the Canadiens immediately and struggled in the limelight for a time, but Robinson was sent to the Nova Scotia Voyageurs for seasoning. Arriving at his first professional training camp at 193 pounds, Robinson, who was 6-foot-4, was told that he had work to do. With effort, he played most of his career between 215 and 220 pounds.

Robinson was called up to Montreal midway through the 1972–73 campaign. Although the Canadiens tried to break him in gently, the rookie defenseman was able to sip champagne from the Stanley Cup for the first time that spring.

Concentrating on the defensive side of his game, Robinson cleared the front of his net with authority. He accumulated his highest penalty totals in his first two complete NHL seasons, partly through the mistakes that any young defenseman makes but also by establishing a presence. It took several more years before he really settled into the kind of game he enjoyed most: hard-hitting but clean. After Robinson took apart the Philadelphia Flyers' notorious pugilist Dave "The Hammer" Shultz in the 1976 Stanley Cup final, his reputation was forged, and he rarely had to brandish his fists again.

The Canadiens won four consecutive championships (1976–79), and Robinson, Serge Savard and Guy Lapointe — Montreal's trio of All-Star defensemen known as "The Big Three" — were key contributors. Robinson emerged as an offensive threat as well as one of "the trees in front of the net" that Boston coach Don Cherry cited as key to Montreal's domination of the Bruins in the Stanley Cup playoffs. While his main asset was his passing, Robinson often surprised opposing teams by using his size

AWARDS: 1st All-Star (3), 2nd All-Star (3), Norris (2), Smythe, Stanley Cup (6), HHOF 1995
STATS:

	GP	G	A	Pts	PIM
RS	1,384	208	750	958	793
PO	227	28	116	144	211

and long reach to carry the puck right to the goalmouth.

He won the first of two Norris Trophies as the NHL's premier defender and the first of five consecutive All-Star selections, with a career-high 19 goals and 66 assists, over the 1976–77 season. In the spring of 1978, Robinson notched 4 goals and 17 assists, tying regular-season scoring-champion Guy Lafleur for most playoff points, and won the Conn Smythe Trophy. In 1986 he won his sixth Stanley Cup ring with another All-Star season under his belt. Then, in 1989, after 17 years in Montreal, it was time for a change.

Robinson concluded his Hockey Hall of Fame–playing career in 1992, after three seasons with the Los Angeles Kings and with 20 consecutive playoff appearances on the record books. He was lured back into the NHL as assistant coach of the New Jersey Devils, who won the Stanley Cup in 1995. He then took the head coaching job with Los Angeles for four seasons before rejoining the Devils as an assistant in 1999–2000.

In a stunning move, Robinson was promoted to head coach with only eight games left in the season. He guided the team to another Cup win, an event he described as "my greatest day in hockey."

When the team faltered in 2001–02, Robinson accepted a demotion back to assistant coach. He had his name etched on the Stanley Cup for the ninth time when New Jersey won again in 2003.

EDDIE SHORE

Fort Qu'Appelle, Saskatchewan
November 25, 1902–
March 16, 1985

NHL CAREER

1926–40 Boston,
NY Americans

They called him the "Edmonton Express" and "Mr. Hockey" until that title was usurped by a more modern legend named Gordie Howe, but "Old Blood and Guts" remains this defenseman's most apt epithet. Over the course of his career, Eddie Shore took 978 stitches to his body. His nose was broken 14 times and his jaw five, and he lost every tooth in his head. His back was fractured, his hip broken and his collarbone cracked. His eyes were frequently blackened, and he suffered cuts to his eyeballs. And every wound dramatically embellished Shore's reputation as the toughest player in hockey. Several wild seasons as a minor-league professional earned Shore an invitation to the Boston Bruins' training camp in 1926. Veteran tough guy Billy Coutu took an immediate dislike to the newcomer and, in a bull-like rush down the ice, slammed into the significantly smaller Shore at full speed. Coutu hit the ice semiconscious, while Shore remained standing, his left ear split from top to bottom and blood gushing onto his face.

When the Bruins' doctor warned Shore that his ear would have to be amputated, Shore found someone willing to stitch up the wound instead. Shore kept his ear, and Boston had a player to be reckoned with.

He played his first NHL game on November 16,

1926, and finished the season with 12 goals — second among NHL defensemen. His penalty total of 130 minutes was second in the league. He followed up his rookie campaign with a total of 165 penalty minutes (an NHL record that lasted for seven years) and 11 goals, tops for defensemen that 1927–28 season.

Shore had become a dynamic skater, with a low crouch and a long, flowing stride. He was as hard-hitting as ever, but his stickhandling made him a constant offensive threat as well. At the end of the 1930–31 season, Shore was named to the NHL's First All-Star Team, as he was six times after that. For the 1933–34 season, however, he was selected only to the Second All-Star Team, probably the result of his 16-game suspension for hitting Ace Bailey from behind at full speed on December 12, 1933. Shore himself suffered a head injury when Toronto's Red Horner dropped him to the ice with an uppercut even as Bailey writhed on the ice — Shore wore

AWARDS: 1st All-Star (7), 2nd All-Star, Hart (4), Stanley Cup (2), HHOF 1947

STATS:

	GP	G	A	Pts	PIM
RS	550	105	179	284	1,047
PO	55	7	12	19	181

a helmet for the rest of his playing career. However, the incident brought Bailey's hockey career to an end and also left an indelible black mark on Shore's Hockey Hall of Fame career.

Shore won four Hart Trophies in the 1930s, as the league's most valuable player. He lead his team to a Stanley Cup victory in the spring of 1939, and then he made the bold decision to buy the Springfield Indians of the International Hockey League. As a result, Shore's NHL contract was traded to the New York Americans, where he agreed to play all their games and as many games for Springfield as he could.

That 1939–40 season was Shore's last in the NHL. He played one more season for Springfield before moving into management full-time, where he quickly became notorious for his penny-pinching and bizarre training methods. He "cured" goaltender Don Simmons of falling to the ice by tying his arms to the crossbar; he also introduced tap dancing in the dressing room and ballet steps on the ice to "improve balance, the foundation of an athlete's ability." When he died in 1985, Shore made sports headlines one last time — with colorful obituaries. Former player Kent Douglas claimed, "Studying with Shore was like getting your doctorate in hockey science," yet for each flattering comment, there were several more stories highlighting his eccentricities and meanness.

DEFENSEMEN
LIONS

Drew Doughty 132
Mike Green.................................... 134
Kris Letang 136
Ryan Suter.................................... 138
Shea Weber.................................... 140

DREW DOUGHTY

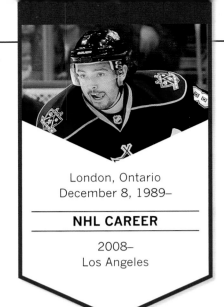

London, Ontario
December 8, 1989–

NHL CAREER

2008–
Los Angeles

Drew Doughty has a thing about numbers. At first he was drawn to the auspicious No. 99, which he wore as a kid, playing hockey in his hometown of London, Ontario. A simple tribute to his hero from nearby Brantford, Doughty, like thousands of young players, idolized Wayne Gretzky. "The Great One" hung up his skates in 1999, and Gretzky's sweater number was retired throughout the NHL. Doughty switched to No. 19 for his other favourite player, Joe Sakic, a center like Gretzky. In junior hockey, and now as a defenseman with the Los Angeles Kings, Doughty chose No. 8 — of personal significance because he was born on December 8 — and a number that's also landed him the nickname "Doughnuts" (because of his surname, the fact that the numeral "8" looks like two stacked doughnuts and as a dig about his somewhat pudgy face). But the numbers most often associated with Doughty have to do with his age, since he has proven himself to be a precocious player, accomplishing much in hockey for a young man.

Doughty won a gold medal with the Canadian team and was voted best defenseman at the 2008 World Junior Championship. As a member of the Guelph Storm, he was twice voted the Ontario League's top defenseman and was

drafted in the first round of the NHL entry draft (second overall), by the Kings, in 2008. A Los Angeles fan since childhood, Doughty was thrilled to don a Kings uniform at the 2008–09 training camp, but he was almost overwhelmed when he made the team at age 18. Few teenagers have success in the NHL, but Doughty not only showed enough speed, skill and poise to make the NHL's All-Rookie Team, he earned a berth with Canada at the 2009 World Championship. He won a silver medal and began to get serious consideration from those assembling Canada's 2010 Olympic Team.

Doughty, a smooth-skating offensive juggernaut with a strong point shot and solid defensive instincts, continued to improve his game during his sophomore season; he turned 20 and made the NHL's 2009–10 Second All-Star Team. The only defenseman to have reached that height at a younger age is Bobby Orr (who accomplished the feat at 19).

"Drew's strengths are poise and defensive acumen — that is the ability to know when to jump up in the rush, the ability to know when to stay back, when to join the rush late and when to lead the rush," noted Bob McKenzie of TSN. However, one could argue that Doughty hit his highest peak to date midway through that season.

Doughty woke up from a sleepless, nerve-wracked night on December 30, 2009, to learn he was the youngest player named to Canada's Olympic hockey team. He proved to be one of Canada's best blueliners at the Games and came home with Olympic gold. Back in the NHL, he led all defensemen in game-winning goals (five), was second in power-play points (31) and third in points (59). Doughty had 16 goals with a plus-20 rating in 82 games and was a finalist for the Norris Trophy.

Doughty helped the Kings back to the playoffs for the first time since 2002, and he found himself back in Vancouver, where the Olympics had been held a scant few months earlier. "To come back to the place where we won that gold medal to play my first Stanley Cup playoff game of my life, well, that's just perfect." said Doughty. "It's going to be one of the big memories of my life. I'm pumped to play here again. I've got some really good memories from here."

Unfortunately, the Kings fell to the powerful Canucks in six games, but not before Doughty

AWARDS:	2nd All-Star				
STATS:					
	GP	G	A	Pts	PIM
RS	239	33	93	126	178
PO	12	5	6	11	12

had tallied three goals and four assists. "He's young, but he's so composed," said veteran teammate Ryan Smyth. "He's not afraid to make mistakes. And he can really change the momentum of a game with his skill. It's not very often you're going to see a defenseman that good at that age."

Like Orr and most stars, Doughty has also had to take some heavy hits, including some borderline ones. In October 2010, he suffered an "upper-body injury" when he took a hard, late hit from Carolina Hurricanes forward Erik Cole. Early that November, Doughty was cleared to return to the Kings lineup after missing six games with an apparent concussion. Even with his decent size — 6 feet and pushing 220 pounds — some said Doughty needed to take his physical game up a notch, but it's his cerebral approach that makes his physical skills such a potent force.

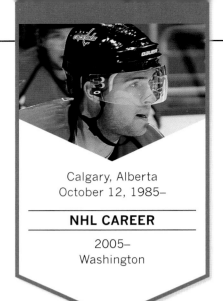

Calgary, Alberta
October 12, 1985–

NHL CAREER

2005–
Washington

MIKE GREEN

Mike Green played his first NHL game in 2005, on the day he turned 20. Less than two years later, he was being talked about in the same breath as Hockey Hall of Famer Paul Coffey and touted as his generation's great offensive defenseman.

Green, from Calgary, had worked his way through the Western Hockey League, with five full seasons with the Saskatoon Blades, to the American Hockey League, playing two partial seasons with the Hershey Bears, to the NHL, with the Washington Capitals. At age 22, he proved the comparisons with Coffey apt when, in the 2007–08 season, he scored 18 goals to become the youngest player since Coffey to lead all NHL defensemen in that category. With fellow Capital Alex Ovechkin, Green became half of the first pair of teammates to lead the NHL in overall goals and goals by a defenseman since Coffey and Mario Lemieux in 1988–89.

Both Green and Ovechkin were selected by the Capitals in the first round of the 2004 entry draft. When Bruce Boudreau took over the Washington coaching duties from the more defensive-minded Glen Hanlon in 2007–08, Green had a breakout season. "My first couple of years with the Capitals, they definitely tried to steer me away from playing offensively or making any types of plays," said Green. "As an offensive-minded guy, it really limited what I could do and, therefore, I wasn't very effective."

Green joined Ovechkin as a fan favorite in Washington, not only because of his goal-scoring ability, but also because of his unique style on and off the ice. He gained the nickname Mike "Game Over" Green with a flurry of exciting game-winning goals. An unofficial fan club sprung up dressed in green at home games — Gang Green — and his signature "faux hawk" hairstyle started a fan frenzy called "Rawk the Hawk" with a local radio station. Even babies were spotted around the DC area sporting mohawks and supporting the Caps. More importantly, with Green's help, the Capitals made the playoffs for the first time since 2003. Green earned league-wide attention and finished seventh in the NHL's Norris Trophy voting.

Green improved his ranking and was the Norris Trophy runner-up in 2008–09. He scored 31 times, only the eighth defenseman in NHL history to reach the 30-goal plateau. Along the way, he broke the NHL record for most consecutive games with a goal by a defenseman (eight) and beat the Washington Capitals record for the most power-play goals in a single season by a defenseman (18, one shy of the NHL record). He made the NHL's First All-Star Team, although some saw him as defensively weak, a charge Paul Coffey also faced for much of his career. He earned consideration for, but not a berth on, Canada's 2010 Olympic hockey team, and even Green acknowledged the need to refine his approach, saying "I really took it upon myself to be better defensively and complete my game, but I'm still young and learning and there are things I have to develop."

Later, he told NHL.com, "The [offensive numbers] are nice, but not something where I can hang my hat and feel like I've accomplished something. I think there's a lot more to accomplish. The thing is, I am looked upon to score goals and create offense from the back end. But I'm trying to become a complete player — that's what I'm striving for."

Unlike many hockey players, who strapped on skates as soon as they could walk, Green didn't start playing until the comparatively older age of 10. Growing up in a working-class family, his parents didn't have a lot of extra money for competitive sports. However, once he was finally able to get onto the ice, he quickly excelled at the sport, and scouts were starting to take notice by the time he was 14.

Today, Green supports "Green's Gang" by purchasing a group of season tickets and donating them to children. At every Capitals home game, he's cheered on by kids who are selected to attend based on need. Since 2008, Green has also been a partner in a charity called "So

Kids Can," and every point he scores generates a donation to help Washington-area children receive prosthetic care. "I just want kids to be happy," said Green. "Playing on the playground or having a playroom when you're in the hospital, it just puts smiles on kids' faces."

AWARDS: 1st All-Star (2)

STATS:

	GP	G	A	Pts	PIM
RS	366	79	165	244	286
PO	36	5	20	8	47

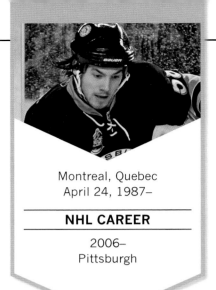

KRIS LETANG

Montreal, Quebec
April 24, 1987–

NHL CAREER

2006–
Pittsburgh

Advancing to the Stanley Cup final as an NHL rookie should have been the experience of a lifetime for Kris Letang. But in the middle of the excitement, the young Pittsburgh Penguins defenseman was dealt a blow that was a harsh reminder about how fleeting life can be.

Letang was just 21 years old when the Penguins made it all the way to the 2008 Stanley Cup final against the Detroit Red Wings. The team had fallen behind 2–0 in the series, and then Letang learned that his best friend, Luc Bourdon, had been killed in a motorcycle accident in his native New Brunswick. The death of Bourdon, a big, promising defense prospect for the Vancouver Canucks, sent shockwaves through the hockey world. Letang had experienced so much with Bourdon, as the two had played together with the Quebec League's Val d'Or Foreurs and had won two gold medals together with Team Canada at the World Junior Championship. Letang left the Stanley Cup final in order to attend the visitation for his fallen friend. "Yes, hockey is important, but when you have a friend like that and you lose him, it's more important than anything," Letang told the Vancouver *Province*. "He helped me with everything, my game, my life." Moving forward, Letang was able to maintain his focus on his

hockey career and he has blossomed into one of the best young defensemen in the game.

In the summer of 2010, the Penguins revamped their entire defense corps, letting long-time standout Sergei Gonchar leave via free agency and signing former New Jersey Devil Paul Martin to bolster the blueline. When the dust settled, Letang established himself as the centerpiece of a new-and-improved group of defensemen.

Letang's first big strides came during the 2008–09 campaign, during which he netted 10 goals and 33 points. He then added four goals and 13 points in 23 playoff games, as the Penguins avenged their loss to Detroit a season earlier by winning a 7-game series to claim the Stanley Cup.

As good as Letang was, there was still a sense that he had yet to reach his full potential. During the 2010–11 season, with increased responsibility as a team leader both on the ice and in the dressing room, he showed everyone just what he is capable of. Letang

AWARDS: Stanley Cup
STATS:

	GP	G	A	Pts	PIM
RS	299	29	100	129	203
PO	59	9	17	26	54

put up 50 points while playing all 82 games for the Penguins, tying for seventh in the league in scoring among defensemen. He also averaged a team-high 24:02 of ice time per game, providing big minutes for a Penguins squad that played much of the year without injured stars Sidney Crosby and Evgeni Malkin.

Letang is listed as a 6-foot, 201–pound defenseman, but that's a generous assessment. Because of his relative lack of size, he doesn't play an overly physical game, but that doesn't mean he's not effective defensively. Positioning is key when manning the blueline, and Letang always seems to know where to be. He also has a knack for getting the puck to the right man when the Penguins are trying to break out of their own zone. His vision and passing skills are a big asset on the attack, where he can quarterback the power play by either distributing the puck or letting go a hard, accurate shot from the blueline.

Like Penguins goalie Marc-André Fleury, Letang can often be seen grinning on the bench or in the dressing room. He seems to have a real sense of how lucky he is. That light attitude, though, shouldn't be mistaken for a lack of intensity. He's a fierce competitor who wants to win as much as anybody.

With the collection of young stars the Penguins have gathered, there's no telling how many championships the team can win over the next few years. With Crosby and Malkin leading the way up front, Letang will be counted on to be the lynchpin of the defense while contributing more offense with his creativity. And you have to believe, given everything he has gone through after losing a best friend, he will truly cherish whatever highs await him.

RYAN SUTER

Madison, Wisconsin
January 21, 1985–

NHL CAREER

2005–
Nashville

If there was a meter tracking family-specific ice time over the past two generations, the Suters of Madison, Wisconsin, would be high on the list. Over the 2009–10 campaign, Ryan Suter led the Nashville Predators in average ice time for the second straight season, posting the third-highest average in franchise history (23:58). He played the 13th-most minutes in the NHL (1,966:02), logging at least 20 minutes in 81 of 82 games. He played in all 82 games for the second consecutive season in 2009–10, and for the third time in four campaigns. He then entered 2010–11 having played 203 consecutive contests, though a knee injury cost him 11 games early in the season. At the 2010 Winter Olympics in Vancouver, he was alternate caption of Team U.S.A., where he led the U.S. in average ice time for the tournament (22:50), highlighted by a game-high 31:31 in the gold-medal game, winning the silver medal.

And that's just Ryan's story. His father, Bob Suter — a member of the 1980 "Miracle on Ice" U.S. Olympic Team — played for the minor-league Nashville South Stars and the University of Wisconsin. His uncle Gary Suter was the NHL's Rookie of the Year in 1986 and enjoyed a distinguished 17-year career on NHL bluelines, and his uncle John Suter also played at Wisconsin. All told, that's evidence of superior

hockey bloodlines — and a lot of skating.

Ryan Suter has been able to parlay his commitment to the game into some impressive accomplishments. He is the king of making the clutch assist in Nashville, ranking first on the team in 2009–10 power-play helpers (15), tying a career high, and third in man-advantage points (17). He plays an excellent all-around game and unleashes a heavy point shot. Suter is also heavy with the body. At 6-foot-1 and nearly 200 pounds, he loves to hit people but spends little time in the penalty box. He launches himself into the fray, and in 2009–10, Suter ranked second amongst the Predators with a career-high 112 blocked shots.

Ryan Suter loved growing up in hockey-mad Madison and has enjoyed playing for his country at every stage of his hockey development. Wearing No. 20, same as his dad and uncle Gary, he's represented the United States at the Under-17, Under-18, Under-20 and senior World Championships. "I feel it's an honour to wear the Team U.S.A. jersey," he said upon being named

STATS:	GP	G	A	Pts	PIM
RS	463	31	161	192	366
PO	29	3	6	9	18

to the 2010 Olympic Team. "And every time I'm on the ice I play my hardest and give everything I have. Playing for Team U.S.A. is one of those things you look forward to. When I got the call and was asked to play on this team, it was an easy answer."

As an amateur, Suter helped the United States capture its first-ever gold medal at the World Junior Championship (WJC), in 2004. He then served as captain for Team U.S.A. at the 2005 WJC (his third consecutive year with the team) and was named to the All-Tournament Team after leading the competition's defensemen in scoring, with one goal and eight points. He also appeared in a contest with Team U.S.A. at the 2005 World Championship in Austria. Suter won U.S.A. Hockey's 2003 Bob Johnson Award, given annually to the U.S. player who excels in international competition, for his efforts at the 2003 WJC. He was the only member of the National Team Development Program to win two gold medals in one season in 2002, when he won gold at the U-18 and U-17 World Championships. He earned best defenseman honors at the 2002 U-18 World Championship in Slovakia and tied as the tournament's top-scoring defenseman. Suter also laced up for the U.S. Select U-18 team at the 2001 Four Nations Cup in the Czech Republic, and he was selected to play in the 2001 U.S.A. Hockey Select-16 tournament.

His family pedigree and strong international play ensured Suter caught the eye of NHL scouts, and in 2003 he was drafted seventh overall

by Nashville. He's fully enjoyed his time in Nashville, as he has always loved fishing, country music and golf when he's not on the ice. In 2008, Suter signed a four-year contract extension for $14 million, and he continues to log large amounts of ice time with a career-high average of 25:12 in the 2010–11 season.

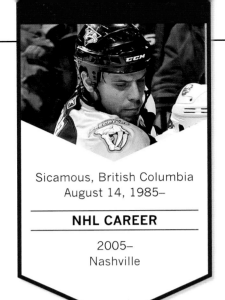

Sicamous, British Columbia
August 14, 1985–

NHL CAREER

2005–
Nashville

SHEA WEBER

Hockey fans and pundits like to play games that often start with a question along the lines of, "If you could pick one defenseman to headline your blueline for the next 10 years, who would it be?" Given the presence of young blueline stars like the Los Angeles Kings' Drew Doughty or Tyler Myers of the Buffalo Sabres, there's no shortage of options for this hypothetical exercise. However, when you factor in everything it takes to be a great defenseman in the league, the name of Nashville Predator captain Shea Weber should come to mind.

Weber looks like he was born to play the game. At 6-foot-4 and 234 pounds he's an imposing figure who can drive opposing forwards into the boards and clear the front of the net. And you have to admire the willingness of anybody, teammates included, to stand in front of the net when he's winding up and putting all of that strength behind a slapshot.

A native of Sicamous, British Columbia, Weber carved out a wonderful junior career with the Kelowna Rockets, a Western League club that's turned out a number of great defensemen recently, including Myers and Toronto Maple Leafs' Luke Schenn. Weber helped lead the powerhouse Rockets to three consecutive Memorial Cup appearances from 2003 to 2005,

and the team skated off with the 2004 title.

Weber, who was taken in the second round of the loaded 2003 NHL draft by the Predators, also added a gold medal from the 2005 World Junior Championship to his résumé before jumping to the NHL. After splitting his time between the Predators and the AHL's Milwaukee Admirals in 2005–06, Weber became a full-time NHLer for the 2006–07 campaign. He showed glimpses of his enormous potential that season by firing 17 goals in 79 games, the fifth-highest total among defensemen.

The following year, Weber was limited to just 54 games due to injury, but he rebounded to net 23 goals — tied for second among blueliners in the NHL — during the 2008–09 season. He was now firmly established as one of the best and most feared up-and-coming players in the league.

Because he plays in Nashville, rather than on a more prominent team, Weber doesn't always garner the attention he might otherwise receive.

AWARDS: 1st All-Star

STATS:

	GP	G	A	Pts	PIM
RS	402	80	134	214	323
PO	33	8	9	17	28

Along with fellow defenseman Ryan Suter, he has helped the Predators play a defensively tight game while always finding a way to scratch out enough goals to remain competitive with every club in the league.

His profile got a lot bigger after he suited up for Canada at the 2010 Olympics Games in Vancouver. A number of young defensemen made the club, and Weber certainly proved he belonged with the world's best, scoring two goals and six points in seven games as the red and white claimed the gold medal.

In the summer of 2010, after Jason Arnott was traded to the New Jersey Devils, Weber was given the captain's "C," which many had predicted would be coming his way. Predators GM David Poile noted Weber's characteristics embody what the entire franchise is about, "In addition to being one of the top young defenseman in the league today, Shea is a natural leader, and we are confident he has the respect of his teammates, opponents, the Predators organization and its fans. He becomes the first Predators draft pick to be named captain and has been part of the culture and belief system we have worked hard to create."

At the 2011 NHL All-Star Game in Carolina, Weber went head to head with behemoth Boston Bruins defenseman Zdeno Chara in the hardest shot competition. Chara eventually won by blasting a shot that registered a record-setting 105.9 miles per hour, but Weber's top offering of 104.8 miles per hour wasn't far off.

A strong second half to the 2010–11 campaign allowed Weber to post 48 points as he continued his evolution into one of the very best defensemen in the game. When you consider the fact there really isn't any one thing Weber can't do on the ice, it's easy to see why so many teams would love to have him on their blueline. With a shot that's as big as his body, the future is now for one of hockey's true all-around stars.

GOALTENDERS
LEGENDS

Johnny Bower.....................................144

Frank Brimsek...................................146

Turk Broda.......................................148

Martin Brodeur 150

Ken Dryden.....................................152

Bill Durnan 154

Grant Fuhr 156

Glenn Hall.......................................158

Dominik Hasek................................160

Bernie Parent...................................162

Jacques Plante...............................164

Patrick Roy......................................166

Terry Sawchuk................................168

Billy Smith.......................................170

Vladislav Tretiak.............................172

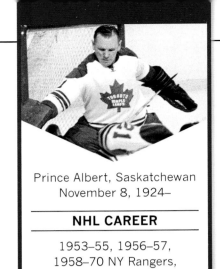

Prince Albert, Saskatchewan
November 8, 1924–

NHL CAREER

1953–55, 1956–57,
1958–70 NY Rangers,
Toronto

JOHNNY BOWER

It's difficult to picture Johnny Bower as a young man, much less a boy. His wizened face, unmasked until his final season, was almost as creased and laugh-lined when he entered the league at the age of 29 as it was when he retired at 45. Bower added hundreds more scars over the span of his career, but he accepted them as an occupational hazard. "I just made up my mind I was going to lose teeth and have my face cut to pieces," he said in explaining his decision to become a goalie. "It was easy."

Bower's real age was the subject of some debate, since he had lied about it in order to join the army during World War II. Amazingly, the four-year war veteran was still eligible to play junior hockey when he returned to civilian life. Bower spent a season back home in Prince Albert, Saskatchewan, then joined the Cleveland Barons in the American Hockey League in 1945.

The New York Rangers gave him his first shot at the big time in the 1953–54 season.

Goaltender Chuck Rayner, who had just retired, gave the rookie goalie tips on his stickwork, particularly the poke check. It would become Bower's signature move.

Acquitting himself admirably that season with New York, Bower played every minute of every game. He had five shutouts on a team that finished out of the playoffs, posting a 2.60 goals-against average. But the Rangers brought in goalie Gump Worsley and gave Bower a ticket back to the minors.

Bower spent the 1954–55 season with Vancouver in the Western Hockey League. A five-game call-up to the Rangers that year went well, but Bower was soon back in the AHL. He played only a couple of NHL games in 1956–57 but racked up numerous AHL awards. He played brilliantly against the Springfield Indians in the 1958 playoffs. Fortuitously, the Indians were managed by Punch Imlach, soon to be installed as manager and coach of the Toronto Maple Leafs. It was just the break Bower needed.

Almost 34 years old when he was drafted by the Maple Leafs in 1958, Bower initially shared duties with Ed Chadwick before

AWARDS: 1st All-Star, Vezina (2), Stanley Cup (4), HHOF 1976

STATS:

	GP	W	L	M	GA	SO	AVE
RS	552	250	195	32,016	1,340	37	2.51
PO	74	35	34	4,378	180	5	2.47

establishing himself as Toronto's number-one — and only — goaltender for the next three years. He spent hours perfecting his poke check. Jabbing his stick with his arm outstretched — often after making a spectacular dive to cover more distance and exercise the element of surprise — Bower could knock the puck off his opponent's stick so his teammates could clear it out of harm's way. He won the Vezina Trophy and First All-Star Team honors in 1960–61.

As genial a player as any who has ever skated in the NHL, Bower was also extremely competitive. "I always played best under pressure," he said. "Maybe it was the money and prestige that went with the big games."

With Bower, Toronto won three consecutive Stanley Cups in the early 1960s. The icing on the cake was the shutout he registered in Game 7 of the 1964 Stanley Cup final. Opposite him in the Detroit Red Wings goal was the legendary Terry Sawchuk, who was traded to Toronto for the 1964–65 season.

Sawchuk and Bower made a potent team. They shared the Vezina Trophy in 1965, and their success prompted the NHL to institute a new rule requiring every club to dress two goalies for every game.

"I wasn't all that glad to see the two-goalie system come in," maintained Bower. "I wanted to play in all the games I possibly could." But the two veterans tag-teamed to a surprising victory for Toronto in the 1967 Stanley Cup final.

Bower retired after the 1968–69 campaign at age 44, but he was persuaded to suit up for one more game the following season. He scouted for the Maple Leafs for 20 years and still runs the Johnny Bower Goaltending School, where students — prompted by parents and grandparents — still ask him to teach them the poke check.

Eveleth, Minnesota
September 26, 1915–
November 11, 1998

NHL CAREER

1938–43, 1945–50
Boston, Chicago

FRANK BRIMSEK

"Usually when the Bruins entered, there would be a lot of cheering," recalled goaltender Frank Brimsek, looking back at a game against the Montreal Canadiens in the Forum on December 1, 1938. "But when I hit the ice, things were so quiet that I could hear the people breathing. They were just waiting for me to blow one."

Earlier in the season, Brimsek had made a quiet rookie debut in the Boston net as a temporary substitute for the legendary "Tiny" Thompson. After missing only two games due to an eye infection, Thompson returned, but Brimsek had obviously made a huge impression on Boston's management. A month later, Boston sold Thompson to Detroit.

Several players, including the levelheaded Dit Clapper, threatened to quit, convinced they'd never win without Thompson. Not only was Brimsek American-born, his parents were Slovenian immigrants. How could he ever succeed?

Brimsek lost his first test against Montreal 2–0, and the fans were on him throughout. But Brimsek shut out his opponents in the next three games, posted another victory and followed that with three more consecutive shutouts. "Kid Zero" — soon to become "Mr. Zero," a name he'd be known by for the

remainder of his career — received standing ovations from the Bruin faithful for the rest of the season. Brimsek's 1.56 goals-against average (GAA) earned him the Vezina and Calder Trophies, and he became the first rookie to make the First All-Star Team. He lowered his GAA to 1.50 in the playoffs to help Boston win the Stanley Cup for the first time in 10 years.

Brimsek anchored the league's best team for the following two years, and Boston won the Cup again in 1941. "He's as quick as a cat," said New York Rangers manager Lester Patrick. "And trying to get him to make the first move is like pushing over [the] Washington Monument."

Detroit goalie Johnny Mowers added, "He's got the best left hand in the business, and nobody plays the angles as well as he does."

Constantly looking for an "edge on the offense," Brimsek also played a sharp mental game. "I always tried to make the opposition player do what I wanted him to," he explained. "I always felt that the glove side was the strongest side for a goaltender. And I would make the shooter believe this too. In that way, I would make most shooters fire the puck to my stick side, which is what I wanted them to do in the first place."

In 1943, Brimsek joined the U.S. Coast Guard. He spent some time tending goal for the Coast

AWARDS: 1st All-Star (2), 2nd All-Star (6), Calder, Vezina (2), Stanley Cup (2), HHOF 1966

STATS:

	GP	W	L	M	GA	SO	AVE
RS	514	252	182	31,210	1,404	40	2.70
PO	68	32	36	4,395	186	2	2.54

Guard Clippers; he then endured 18 months of active duty in the South Pacific with a Coast Guard supply ship. The experience changed him profoundly. "I came back too soon after being in the service," admitted Brimsek. "My nerves were jumpy. I should have taken a rest before coming back, but I needed the money."

He returned to the NHL midway through the 1945–46 season, but his playing days were numbered. "When I got out of the war, I knew I wasn't going to play long. I didn't have that same feeling for the game," he said. "I had a hard time even going back to training camp." Yet Maurice "Rocket" Richard, who became a league star during Brimsek's military leave, called Brimsek "the toughest goalie I ever faced."

Brimsek made the Second All-Star Team three years in a row. Meanwhile, he was preparing for retirement. "I had spoken to [general manager] Art Ross in 1947 and told him that I would like to leave Boston in '49 to go to Chicago," said Brimsek. "My brother was starting a business there, and I thought I might help him open a few doors. Ross agreed, but when it came time, he didn't like the idea anymore. 'If that's the way you feel,' I told him, 'I'll quit altogether!'"

Brimsek got his trade to Chicago, and, even with the last-place Black Hawks, he added five more career shutouts in his final NHL season, in 1950. In 1966, he was elected to the Hockey Hall of Fame.

Brandon, Manitoba
May 15, 1914–
October 17, 1972

NHL CAREER

1936–43, 1945–52 Toronto

TURK BRODA

"He's the best playoff player in all hockey," claimed Toronto Maple Leafs owner and manager Conn Smythe, and when Turk Broda died in 1972, his record of 13 playoff shutouts still stood.

"The bonus money for winning wasn't much," laughed Broda, "but I always needed it."

Walter Broda earned his nickname as a child, when his class was told the story of an old English king called "Turkey Egg" by his subjects because of his freckles. Since Broda had more freckles than any of his schoolmates, the moniker became his as well. Soon it was just "Turk," and the tag stuck.

Broda turned professional with Detroit's International League farm club in 1935. "He hasn't a nerve in his body," declared Red Wings general manager Jack Adams. "He could play in a tornado and never blink an eye." But in 1936, Smythe acquired the promising netminder for $8,000.

After five strong seasons, Broda won his first Vezina Trophy in 1940–41. The following season, he backstopped his team in the most remarkable comeback in Stanley Cup history. Down three games to none, he allowed only seven goals in the next four contests to help the Maple Leafs to their first championship in 10 years.

By 1945, the next time Toronto won the Stanley Cup, Broda had been in the army for almost two years. A public controversy had erupted when the Royal Canadian Mounted Police stopped his train en route to Montreal, arrested Broda and returned him to Toronto — all so that he would play hockey for the Toronto Army Daggers rather than the Montreal military team, which had offered him a $2,400 bonus. The frustrated Broda would later complain that he had been drafted to stop pucks rather than bullets.

Broda returned to NHL duty late in the 1945–46 season. "We were outplayed and outchanced in scoring opportunities, I would think, by about three to two," said Toronto rookie Howie Meeker. "Turk Broda was the guy who won that series." The Maple Leafs won their first of three consecutive Stanley Cups.

AWARDS: 1st All-Star (2), 2nd All-Star, Vezina (2), Stanley Cup (5), HHOF 1967

STATS:

	GP	W	L	M	GA	SO	AVE
RS	629	302	224	38,167	1,609	62	2.53
PO	101	60	39	6,389	211	13	1.98

Broda's colorful character made him a crowd favorite. Before accepting his teammates' congratulations after a victory, he would rush around the ice scooping up the cigars his fans had showered down. His chubby face and portly build made him an unlikely looking NHL star, and when the Maple Leafs faltered, 35-year-old Broda was an easy target. "If it isn't Turk's fault, we'll find out whose it is," said Smythe after the Maple Leafs stumbled halfway through the 1949–50 season. "I'm taking Broda out of the nets, and he's not going back until he shows some common sense." To back up his threat that the 5-foot-9 Broda wouldn't play until he shed seven of his 197 pounds, Smythe called up a reserve and then traded for up-and-coming netminder Al Rollins. "Two seasons ago, [Turk] weighed 185. Last season, he went up to 190 — and now this," complained Smythe. "A goalie has to have fast reflexes, and you can't move fast when you're overweight."

Broda won the "battle of the bulge" by fasting and sweating his way down to the prescribed weight. He shed a further four pounds while earning a shutout in his first game back. Although Broda played in 31 games, Rollins was awarded the Vezina Trophy for Toronto's 1950–51 season. However, it was Broda who sparkled in eight of the Maple Leafs' 11 playoff games. His minuscule 1.13 goals-against average helped Toronto to another Stanley Cup victory. That series, however, was Broda's swan song: He appeared in only three games the next season before retiring.

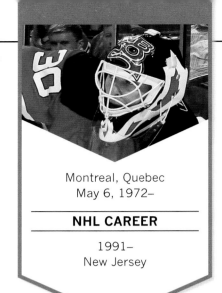

MARTIN BRODEUR

Montreal, Quebec
May 6, 1972–

NHL CAREER

1991–
New Jersey

Martin Brodeur's assault on the NHL record book has been steady, efficient and often spectacular. Terry Sawchuk's record of 103 career regular-season shutouts was believed unassailable, and it was for over three decades. Even while Brodeur was creeping up on Sawchuk's remarkable feat, it was not a foregone conclusion that he would break the record until he notched a career-best 12 shutouts in the 2006–07 season. Then aged 34, it was certain Brodeur had a shot at the shutout crown, arguably the most prestigious of goaltending records. He entered the 2009–10 season only two shutouts shy of the mark, and on December 21, 2009, he set the new standard with 35 saves against the defending Stanley Cup winners in Pittsburgh.

"Tying [the record] was pretty amazing in Buffalo a couple weeks ago," said Brodeur, "and now surpassing it, it's a great honor for me to be in that position. It was almost like winning a playoff game. The guys kept chipping the puck out and everybody was blocking shots everywhere. It was a great effort from my teammates."

Modesty aside, Brodeur has certainly benefited from playing exclusively for the perennially defensive-minded New Jersey Devils. But a shutout represents perfection, and Brodeur has been the backbone of the Devils club for almost 20 years, earning all of the accolades he has received.

Breaking records was not new for Brodeur by that point in his career, as he had already established the career records for regular season wins, appearances and minutes played. To date, he is tied with his former hero Patrick Roy for most career playoff shutouts (23). Named Rookie of the Year in 1993–94, he won his first Stanley Cup ring in 1995, an achievement he repeated in 2000 and 2003. Brodeur won his first Jennings Trophy with partner Mike Dunham in 1997 and his fifth in 2010. He was voted Vezina Trophy winner in 2003, 2004, 2007 and 2008 and has been named to the First or Second All-Star Team seven times.

Brodeur plays a relatively stand-up style of butterfly, has a lightning-fast glove hand and is arguably still the best puck-handling goalie in the league. A teammate only half-jokingly suggested that, despite the encumbrance of today's huge goalie gloves, Brodeur could play point on the New Jersey power play because of the strength of his shot.

In 1995, Brodeur started to speak openly about his desire to score. "I need a goal now," he said. "I'm looking for the chance all the time. If I get it and it doesn't jeopardize my team, I'm going for it."

He came close several times, finally potting a shot when Montreal pulled its goalie for an extra attacker while down two goals late in a 1997 playoff game. Brodeur fired the puck into the vacant cage, and the New Jersey crowd went wild. Brodeur was credited with a Philadelphia "own goal" in February 2000, equaling Ron Hextall's record of two career goals by a netminder.

Brodeur's effectiveness with the puck was part of the reason that, after the lockout, the league instituted measures to limit where goalies could handle the puck. "If you give liberty to the goalies to play the puck," Brodeur argued, "they'll mess up more than they're successful." But he was not convincing.

Brodeur has had a much-decorated international career with Canada. As backup to Patrick Roy in the 1998 Olympics, he saw no action, apparently due to Roy's insistence. Brodeur admitted to harboring a grudge in a 2006 autobiography, but he got his shot at the 2002 Olympics. He started the tourney as a backup, but when Curtis Joseph lost the opening game, Team Canada turned to Brodeur. He went undefeated and returned to the Devils with a gold medal. In 2004, he backstopped Canada to a convincing World Cup win, allowing only five goals in five games.

Brodeur was named Canada's starter at the 2006 Olympics. He played four out of six games but failed to get a medal. At the 2010 games, he was in net for a loss to Team U.S.A. in the preliminary round, and Canada turned to Roberto Luongo for the rest of the tournament. As a supportive teammate, Brodeur collected his second Olympic gold medal. It seems likely younger goalies will henceforth get the nod for Team Canada. Brodeur and the New Jersey Devils experienced some atypical struggles in the 2010–11 season; however, Brodeur's status among the greatest in the game is already firmly established.

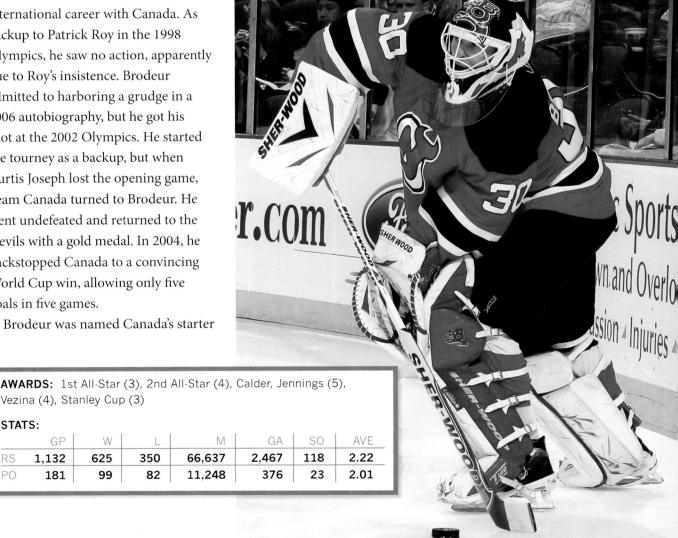

AWARDS: 1st All-Star (3), 2nd All-Star (4), Calder, Jennings (5), Vezina (4), Stanley Cup (3)

STATS:

	GP	W	L	M	GA	SO	AVE
RS	1,132	625	350	66,637	2,467	118	2.22
PO	181	99	82	11,248	376	23	2.01

KEN DRYDEN

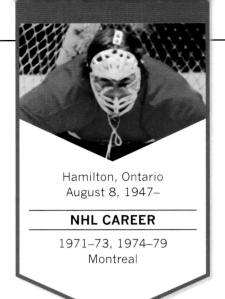

Hamilton, Ontario
August 8, 1947–

NHL CAREER

1971–73, 1974–79
Montreal

In 1972, Ken Dryden took time out from sightseeing with Team Canada to visit the hockey department of the Institute of Physical Culture and Sport in Moscow. The Soviets' scientific approach led one official to insist Dryden was too tall to be a goaltender. "There are disadvantages," the 6-foot-4 Dryden conceded, "but there are advantages too: my reach. I can cover a lot of goal." His host was unconvinced, but NHL shooters knew better. While he played fewer than eight NHL seasons, Dryden was goalie for six Stanley Cup–winning teams, had six All-Star campaigns and never lost more than 10 games in any one campaign.

"The team always felt that [Dryden] could win them a big game if he had to," said coaching legend Scotty Bowman, whose career with the Canadiens began in Dryden's rookie year (1971–72) and ended with his netminder's retirement in 1979. "He was the most consistent goaltender I have ever coached, and a fierce competitor."

Dryden followed his brother Dave's lead. Their first meeting on NHL ice, on March 2, 1971 — with veteran Dave in net for the Buffalo Sabres and call-up Ken guarding Montreal's cage — replicated hundreds of backyard games. However, the brothers had taken radically

different routes to the NHL. Dryden spurned Canadian junior hockey to play four years at Cornell University while working toward a law degree, an unlikely path to the NHL in the 1960s. Although the Montreal Canadiens were interested in his services, Dryden accepted an offer with the Canadian national team that would allow him to continue his education.

When the national team program folded a year later, Dryden entered the Montreal farm system. It wasn't long before he was brought up to the parent club, and he played in the last six games of the 1970–71 season. He won every match and posted a 1.65 goals-against average, but the hockey world was stunned when Montreal started him against the defending Stanley Cup–champion Boston Bruins in the first playoff game that spring.

The Bruins had finished 24 points ahead of the Canadiens that season, but Dryden backstopped the Canadiens to a seven-game upset. He eventually won the Conn Smythe Trophy for his part in vanquishing Minnesota and Chicago en route to a Stanley Cup victory. He proved that it was more than beginner's luck when he won the Calder Trophy the next season, his official rookie year. He earned his second Stanley Cup ring in 1973, but, dissatisfied with his contract, Dryden

AWARDS: 1st All-Star (5), 2nd All-Star, Calder, Smythe, Vezina (5), Stanley Cup (6), HHOF 1983

STATS:

	GP	W	L	M	GA	SO	AVE
RS	397	258	57	23,352	870	46	2.24
PO	112	80	32	6,846	274	10	2.40

shocked fans and pundits alike when he quit the game that year to return to his legal career.

When Montreal faltered badly without Dryden in the 1973–74 season, the club offered to quadruple his salary, raising it to the going rate for the NHL's best talent. The following season, Dryden once again traded his legal pads for goalie pads.

His "leave of absence" had just been part of hard bargaining, and he quickly picked up where he had left off. A year after his return, Dryden backstopped Montreal to four consecutive Stanley Cups.

Dryden's iconic pose — gloves stacked on the butt end of his stick, chin resting on his blocker — was original and unforgettable. While the image epitomized the thinker he is, it was also a ritual that helped him stretch out a long spine that spent too much time in a crouch. Unfortunately, Dryden's back finally got the better of him, and in 1979 he announced his retirement, this time for good.

His book *The Game* launched him into a successful writing and broadcasting career. In 1997, Dryden moved into an executive position with the Toronto Maple Leafs, and in 2004 he was elected to the Canadian parliament. He was re-elected twice, served as a cabinet minister and ran for the Liberal Party leadership. In 2007, Dryden briefly re-entered the hockey arena when the Canadiens retired his No. 29 sweater.

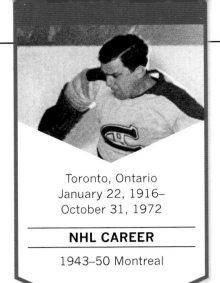

Toronto, Ontario
January 22, 1916–
October 31, 1972

NHL CAREER

1943–50 Montreal

BILL DURNAN

Bill Durnan tended goal with a unique pair of gloves — fingered catching mitts that allowed him to hold his goalie's stick in either hand and to adjust his stance to face an attacker with a catching glove always in the optimum position, covering the wider part of the net. He credited Steve Faulkner, his boyhood coach, with his ambidextrous ability. "He worked me by the hour," explained Durnan, "until I had the technique down pat, and we won five city championships in six years. At first, it felt as though I was transferring a telephone pole from one hand to the other, but after a while, I'd hardly realize I was doing it." Not only ambidextrous, Durnan also had lightning reflexes, particularly in his hands; it was a combination that confounded shooters throughout his career.

Durnan was originally signed in 1936 by the Toronto Maple Leafs. He won junior hockey's Memorial Cup while playing in the Maple Leafs' farm system and was subsequently to go to his first NHL training camp. Unfortunately, just before camp opened, he injured his knee in a playful tussle with a friend. When the Maple Leafs heard about his injury, they immediately dropped him from their protected list.

Durnan angrily vowed never to play in the NHL, even drifting from hockey for a time after his knee healed. Before long, though, he was active in the mercantile leagues, playing goal in the winter and baseball in the summer as a pitcher, always with a guaranteed company job to augment his income. He starred for several teams, including the Kirkland Lake Blue Devils, who won hockey's Allan Cup in 1940 — a prestigious trophy at the time.

During the 1940–41 season, Durnan began keeping net for the Montreal Royals in the Quebec senior league. He was content, but in 1943 he started to feel considerable pressure to play for the Canadiens. "Somehow, I managed to hold out until the day of the opening game," he explained years after he finally gave in. "I signed for the huge sum of $4,200 and found myself on a hockey team just beginning to jell." That season Durnan won the Vezina Trophy and a First

AWARDS: 1st All-Star (6), Vezina (6), Stanley Cup (2), HHOF 1964

STATS:

	GP	W	L	M	GA	SO	AVE
RS	383	208	112	22,945	901	34	2.36
PO	45	27	18	2,871	99	2	2.07

All-Star Team selection, as he would in five of the next six seasons.

Durnan and the rest of the Canadiens slumped badly in the 1947–48 season, and the Montreal fans voiced their displeasure. "They booed me and made me feel six inches high," Durnan lamented. "I don't know whether you've ever heard 13,000 people all calling you the same bad name at the same time, but it sure makes a loud noise." Durnan threatened to quit, but he was persuaded to stay and rebounded with two more excellent seasons.

Durnan looked back at the 1949–50 campaign as "the beginning of the end." He decided to quit after the season's last game. "I'll admit," he conceded in 1972, "if they were paying the kind of money goaltenders get today, they'd have had to shoot me to get me out of the game. But at the end of any given season, I never had more than $2,000 in the bank. I wasn't educated and had two little girls to raise. All this worried me a great deal, and I was also hurting."

Heavily favored Montreal faced New York in the first round of the 1950 playoffs, but the Rangers jumped into a 3–0 lead in games. Durnan decided Gerry McNeil, a promising young goalie pegged as his eventual replacement, might as well start the next game.

While admitting that the emotional turmoil he felt was agonizing, "the nerves and all the accompanying crap," Durnan attested, "were built up." Yet the story went out that Durnan couldn't handle the pressure and had suffered a nervous breakdown. McNeil started game four, and Durnan never played another professional hockey game.

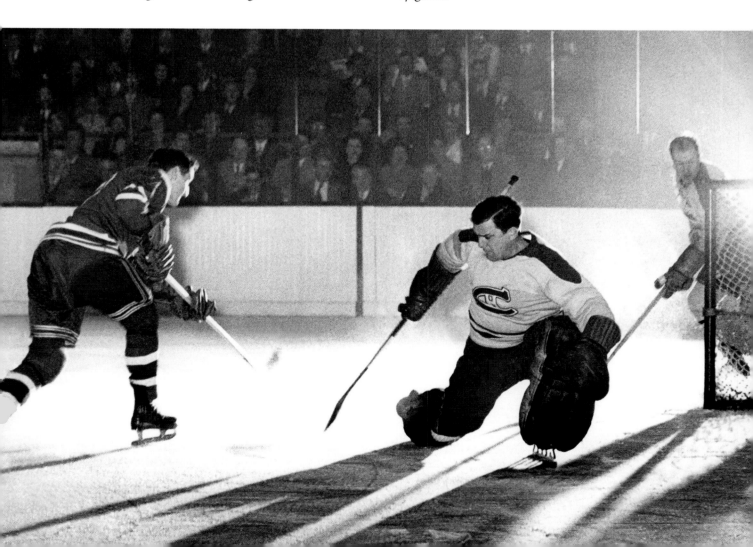

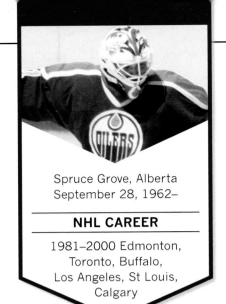

Spruce Grove, Alberta
September 28, 1962–

NHL CAREER

1981–2000 Edmonton,
Toronto, Buffalo,
Los Angeles, St Louis,
Calgary

GRANT FUHR

Grant Fuhr got off to an inauspicious start with the St. Louis Blues, showing up for training camp in 1995 almost 25 pounds overweight. The goalie was immediately sent packing by coach and general manager "Iron Mike" Keenan. Fuhr returned a week later — and 14 pounds lighter. By the beginning of the season, he was down to his regular weight of 200 pounds and back in Keenan's good graces. Fuhr was in net for the first match of that campaign and went on to set an NHL record for goaltenders by starting 79 games in one season — 76 in succession.

The move to St. Louis proved to be a tonic for Fuhr. Following 10 spectacular and glory-filled seasons with the Edmonton Oilers, Fuhr had been traded to the Toronto Maple Leafs in 1991 after publicly acknowledging a drug-abuse problem. He had a decent season with the Maple Leafs, but Felix Potvin also arrived in Toronto that year. Fuhr coached Potvin so well that he was unseated as Toronto's "go-to" goaltender. Early in 1993, the Maple Leafs sent Fuhr to the Buffalo Sabres. Unfortunately for Fuhr, Dominik Hasek was just emerging as a star. While the two shared the William M. Jennings Trophy with the league's lowest goals-against average in the 1993–94 season, Fuhr, as second-stringer, was dealt to the Los Angeles Kings only three games into the

following season. There his average, never his strong suit, ballooned for the first time to more than four goals a game. In the summer of 1995, he arrived in St. Louis as a free agent.

After his initial blowup with Keenan, Fuhr, once again at his acrobatic best with perhaps the league's sharpest reflexes, posted his lowest seasonal average.

"I've often learned things the hard way," said Fuhr, but for the longest time, everything had seemed to come easily to him. His 78–21–1 junior record had prompted Edmonton to use its first-round (eighth overall) draft pick in 1981 to choose him. Midway through his rookie NHL season, at the age of 19, Fuhr became the youngest goalie to play in an NHL All-Star Game. At season's end, he was runner-up in Vezina Trophy voting and selected for the Second All-Star Team. "He was born to be a goaltender," Mark Messier once said. "I'm sure he feels more comfortable in his hockey equipment than he does in his pajamas."

In Edmonton, a power struggle between goalies Fuhr and Andy Moog soon emerged. Both netminders shared regular-season duties, but Fuhr got almost all the calls in the playoffs. "Fuhr is one of the most unflappable athletes I have ever met," said broadcaster Darren Pang, a

former NHL goaltender. "There is no pulse in the most pressurized situations, and that has always been his greatest asset." Fuhr backed the Oilers to four Stanley Cup victories in five years. While Edmonton's run-and-gun style meant the team gave up almost as many scoring opportunities as it created, Fuhr shone under the heavy workload. Although he didn't play the puck as much as many other goalies, he nevertheless set an NHL record in 1983–84 for most points in a season, with 14 assists.

Fuhr used a strong showing for Canada's winning team in the 1987 Canada Cup tournament as a springboard for his best NHL season. When Moog departed in frustration, Fuhr led the league in minutes played en route to his selection to the First All-Star Team and his only Vezina Trophy. He succumbed to his first serious injury two years later, and Bill Ranford stepped into the breach. Healed but on the bench, Fuhr watched his team win the Stanley Cup again in 1990.

During four seasons with the Blues, the injuries started to come more frequently. Fuhr was dealt to the Calgary Flames for the 1999–2000 campaign, but he never truly found his groove there. Fuhr announced his retirement at season's end. In 2003, he entered the Hockey Hall of Fame.

AWARDS: 1st All-Star, 2nd All-Star, Jennings, Vezina, Stanley Cup (4), HHOF 2003

STATS:

	GP	W	L	M	GA	SO	AVE
RS	868	403	295	48,945	2,756	25	3.38
PO	150	92	50	8,834	430	6	2.92

GLENN HALL

Humboldt, Saskatchewan
October 3, 1931–

NHL CAREER

1952–53, 1954–71 Detroit,
Chicago, St. Louis

Records are made to be broken, but goaltender Glenn Hall's record for consecutive games will never be bettered. From the first game of the 1955–56 campaign until 12 games into the 1962–63 season, Hall never missed a minute of NHL action. Finally, on November 7, 1962, Hall pulled himself out of a game against Boston due to back problems. When the Bruins scored on their first shot of the game, Hall went to the bench, conferred briefly with his coach and then headed for the dressing room.

As Hall explained later, "I was able to take a comfortable stance, but I couldn't move with the play when it crossed in front of the net. A goalie who can't do that might as well be up in the stands." Hall's streak ended at 502 games — 552 including playoffs. It remains one of the most remarkable accomplishments in hockey history. Since goalies typically do not play for entire seasons anymore, let alone over 500 games

in a row, Hall's record has a reasonable chance of never being broken.

On October 2, 1955, Hall played for the defending Stanley Cup–champion Detroit Red Wings in his first of a record 13 All-Star games (he had played just eight NHL games before that pre-season game, but he showed such promise that the Red Wings traded away the great Terry Sawchuk). At season's end, Hall led the league in shutouts, a feat he repeated five times, and was voted rookie of the year.

Hall always spoke his mind, a trait that led Detroit general manager Jack Adams to trade him in 1957 to the sad-sack Chicago Black Hawks, along with Players' Association organizer Ted Lindsay. Hall, however, never missed a beat. Four years later, he backstopped the Black Hawks to the Stanley Cup.

Hall knew what worked for him and had the courage to stick with it despite the criticism he faced. He pioneered the butterfly style of goaltending, having discovered that he could cover more of the net and still keep his body upright, ready to spring back to his feet, by crouching and keeping his legs spread

AWARDS: 1st All-Star (6), 2nd All-Star (4), Calder, Smythe, Vezina (3), Stanley Cup, HHOF 1975

STATS:

	GP	W	L	M	GA	SO	AVE
RS	906	407	326	53,484	2,222	84	2.49
PO	115	49	65	6,899	320	6	2.78

below the knees. Protected by better equipment, goalies now spend most of their time fending off attackers while down in the butterfly position. In Hall's day, a goalie who went down too often risked taking a shot in the face. "Back then, the goaltenders always thought survival," Hall said years later. "The styles have changed so much since the mask came in. We tried to get our feet over in front of the puck and the head out of the way. It was survival, number one." Hall himself did not wear a mask until the final two seasons of his career.

Ironically, "Mr. Goalie," as he was called, appeared to hate hockey. He was sick to his stomach before every game and often between periods. "Five minutes before a game or between a period, I didn't hear what a coach was saying because I was in total preparation," recalled Hall. "All I would be thinking about was what I had to do. During a game, when someone got ready to shoot, I'd already looked at the shot in my mind. I tried to prepare myself for every option." Hall's vomit bucket became part of his legend.

Although Chicago retired his number in 1988, in 1967, Black Hawks management deemed Hall expendable. They left the 36-year-old unprotected in the league's first expansion draft, and the St. Louis Blues quickly made him their first selection. Hall was so spectacular while his team was being swept out of the 1968 Stanley Cup final by the Montreal Canadiens that he was awarded the Conn Smythe Trophy as best playoff performer. His lowest goals-against average in the league was recognized with the

Vezina Trophy for a third time when he shared goaltending duties with the even older Jacques Plante in 1968–69, earning a First All-Star Team selection the same season.

Hall finally retired in 1971 at the age of 40. In the years since, only Martin Brodeur has bettered his 84 career shutouts, leaving Hall in fourth place in NHL history.

Pardubice, Czechoslovakia
January 29, 1965–

NHL CAREER

1990–2002, 2003–04,
2005–08 Chicago, Buffalo,
Detroit, Ottawa

DOMINIK HASEK

"Dominik Hasek has proven to be the best player in the world the last two years. " said Wayne Gretzky in 1998, " Not only for what he did for the Buffalo Sabres and for the NHL, but for what he did for his country in the Olympic Games." Hasek unexpectedly took the Czech Republic team into the medal round, eliminating a strong American squad before facing the Canadian favorites in the semifinals.

Hasek nursed a 1–0 lead with dozens of brilliant saves before Canada's Trevor Linden found a chink in Hasek's armor with only a minute left on the clock. Both Hasek and Canadian netminder Patrick Roy were flawless in an overtime period. It was the "most intense pressure of my life," said Hasek, but he blanked all five Canadians during the shootout, while the Czechs managed to slip one by Roy. Facing Russia in the final game, Hasek posted a shutout in a tense 1–0 victory. He went home a national hero, with a gold medal around his neck and an Olympic goals-against average of 0.97.

Chicago had drafted Hasek with the 199th pick in the 1983 NHL entry draft, but Hasek had no interest in coming to North America then. He was the Czech Goaltender of the Year from 1986–90 before joining Chicago's minor league affiliate in Indianapolis in the 1990–91 season. He appeared in five games with the Blackhawks and compiled a 10–4–1 record with the team the following season, making the 1992 NHL All-Rookie Team. Ed Belfour was clearly the number-one goalie in Chicago, and it took a trade to the Buffalo Sabres to convince Hasek not to head home. Within a year, "The Dominator" had established himself as the league's premier goaltender.

Hasek won the Vezina Trophy in his second season as a Sabre and five times after that. His 1.95 goals-against average in 1993–94 marked the first time a goalie had dropped below 2.00 in 20 years. The Hart Trophy, which had not gone to a goaltender since 1962, went to Hasek in both 1997 and 1998, along with the Lester B. Pearson Award.

"He's got an advantage on a lot of shooters because of the reputation he's built up," observed Mats Sundin. "Guys see him in the net and think they have to try something special to score a goal."

"He's done some things nobody's seen before," noted Buffalo coach Lindy Ruff, "dropping his stick and using his other hand, making saves with his head, rolling over and laying his arm on the ice, rolling over and kicking his legs up." Hasek almost single-handedly took the Sabres to the 1999 Stanley Cup final, but he requested a trade to a contender for 2001–02.

Hasek's new team, the Detroit Red Wings, finished first in the league — 18 points ahead of the second-place team. Hasek drank from the Stanley Cup, after contributing six shutouts, and then several months later he confirmed his retirement plans.

After a year off, Hasek missed the game. The Red Wings didn't hesitate to bring him back, but, plagued by a nagging groin injury, Hasek missed most of the 2003–04 campaign. After the NHL lockout the previous season, Hasek joined Ottawa as a free agent in 2005–06. He played strongly but sustained a groin injury in the first game of the 2006 Turin Olympics and didn't play again that season. The Senators, deeply disappointed Hasek hadn't joined them for their playoffs, declined to sign him for the next season.

The Red Wings, again, welcomed Hasek, and he alternated games with Chris Osgood for most of the next two seasons. Hasek got the nod for the 2007 playoffs, but when he faltered early in the 2008 post-season, he watched Osgood backstop the Red Wings to Stanley Cup victory. Hasek, the consummate teammate, celebrated the win before announcing his retirement.

After another season out of the game, Hasek donned his pads once more, leading his hometown Pardubice team to a Czech national title, then he signed a contract at age 45 to play for Moscow Spartak in Russia's Kontinental League for 2010–11.

AWARDS: 1st All-Star (7), Hart (2), Jennings (3), Pearson (2), Vezina (6), Stanley Cup (2)

STATS:

	GP	W	L	M	GA	SO	AVE
RS	735	389	223	42,837	1,572	81	2.20
PO	119	65	49	7,318	246	14	2.02

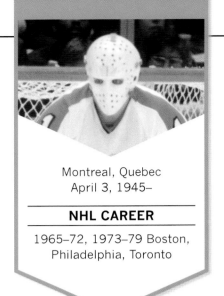

Montreal, Quebec
April 3, 1945–

NHL CAREER

1965–72, 1973–79 Boston,
Philadelphia, Toronto

BERNIE PARENT

"The mask gives you protection, saves you a few hundred stitches," noted Bernie Parent, "but the best thing it does is hide your face from the crowd." Fame rather than shame was behind Parent's desire for concealing his features — the slogan "Only the Lord saves more than Bernie Parent" appeared frequently on signs at games and on bumper stickers all over Philadelphia.

Signed by the Boston Bruins when he was a teenager, Parent got his first big break in Junior A hockey playing for coach Hap Emms in Niagara Falls. "Until I turned 18, I didn't know what a goaltender was supposed to do," he has said. "I just did things by instinct." Emms taught him how to play the angles, and Parent made an auspicious NHL debut in 1965 when both of Boston's starting goalies were injured. "Parent has given this club the lift it needs," said Bruins coach Milt Schmidt. "He has all the moves, he stays up, and he stays remarkably cool."

Although Parent completed a decent rookie year, his play slipped in his second season. "If an athlete ever tells you booing doesn't bother him," said Parent, "he's either in a trance or just plain ignorant." Parent was sent to the minors, and the Philadelphia Flyers made him their first pick in the expansion draft the following summer. He shared duties with Doug Favell for three seasons before being sent to the Toronto Maple Leafs midway through the 1970–71 season.

Though he was initially upset, Parent realized the trade was fortunate when Jacques Plante shook his hand in the dressing room. "Plante was like a god to me," he later recalled. "Now I was on the same team with him."

"We'll be playing together," said Plante warmly, "so just ask if there is anything I can help you with." Parent discovered his idol literally had a book on every shooter in the league and wrote notes on every arena regarding the play of the boards and even the lighting. By the end of the 1971–72 season, Parent had made Plante's scientific goaltending system his own.

The Miami Screaming Eagles of the fledgling World Hockey Association

AWARDS: 1st All-Star (2), Smythe (2), Vezina (2), Stanley Cup (2), HHOF 1984

STATS:

	GP	W	L	M	GA	SO	AVE
RS	608	271	198	35,136	1,493	54	2.55
PO	71	38	33	4,302	174	6	2.43

enticed Parent to jump to the new league in 1972. Miami folded its team before playing a game, and Parent's contract was picked up by the WHA's Philadelphia Blazers. He was ecstatic about returning to Philadelphia, and the heavy barrage of shots he faced in 65 games for the Blazers was just what he needed after Plante's tutoring. But one season in the WHA was enough. The Blazers folded, and Parent managed to force Toronto to trade his NHL rights to the Philadelphia Flyers for the 1973–74 season.

"My first [exhibition] game back with the Flyers was a forgettable one," Parent laughingly recalled. "After 12 minutes, I had let in seven goals." But he notched four shutouts in his first 10 games of the regular season. Parent shared the Vezina Trophy with Chicago's Tony Esposito, and his stingy 2.02 goals-against average in the ensuing playoffs helped the Flyers march to the Stanley Cup final and defeat the favored Boston Bruins. Parent's stellar performance — punctuated with a 1–0 shutout in the clinching game — earned him the Conn Smythe Trophy.

"We know the exhilarating feeling only a player on a Stanley Cup winner can appreciate," he exclaimed after another MVP performance, when the Flyers won their second consecutive Cup. "It won't be easy for any team to take the Cup away." But Montreal swept them in the 1976 final, and Parent never got that close again.

"Once a game starts, I forget about the shots and getting hurt," he said, but Parent was struck down midway through the 1978–79 season. A stick glanced up in a goalmouth scramble and jabbed him in the eye. A sympathetic reaction in the other eye left the goaltender in complete darkness for two weeks.

Fortunately, Parent's sight returned, but his playing career was over. His jersey was officially retired, and he turned his attention to sharing his wisdom with new generations of Philadelphia goalies.

Shawinigan Falls, Quebec
January 17, 1929–
February 27, 1986

NHL CAREER

1952–65, 1968–73 Montreal,
NY Rangers, St. Louis,
Toronto, Boston

JACQUES PLANTE

If Jacques Plante had not stood up to Montreal Canadiens coach Toe Blake on the night of November 2, 1959, the number of career-ending injuries suffered by the sport's goaltenders would be far higher. When sniper Andy Bathgate of the New York Rangers ripped open Plante's nose with a backhand, Plante informed Blake that the only way he would go back in net that night was with his mask on, the one he had worn in practice for years.

With no backup goalie dressed and his team enjoying a 4–1 lead, Blake relented. Plante was allowed to wear the mask until his nose healed. The Canadiens promptly won their next 11 games with a masked man in net. Still, Blake made Plante stick to their agreement, and a healed and barefaced Plante started the next game. The team lost, and Blake let Plante decide whether the mask had helped or hindered his play. Plante's mask went on for good, and the face of goaltending was forever changed.

Ten years later, Plante was able to argue that the mask had saved his life. The 41-year-old was playing excellent goal for the St. Louis Blues in the 1970 Stanley Cup final when a rising puck caught him just above the left eye, putting him out of the series with a concussion but without a cut or fracture. Without the mask, said Plante, "I would have been dead. No question."

Plante was as eccentric in life as he was brilliant in goal. He found knitting relaxing and made the tuques he liked to wear in net (he claimed they spared him a chill). Denied this comfort by Blake, who didn't like the look of it, Plante knit undershirts instead. An asthmatic, he often complained about breathing problems in certain locations and occasionally stayed in a different hotel from that of his teammates. This further distanced him from those who saw camaraderie as integral to success.

Plante was a private man off the ice and egotistical to boot, but he was the ultimate team player on the ice. He constantly called out helpful advice to his teammates and was the first goalie to signal impending icing

AWARDS: 1st All-Star (3), 2nd All-Star (4), Hart, Vezina (7), Stanley Cup (6), HHOF 1978

STATS:

	GP	W	L	M	GA	SO	AVE
RS	837	437	246	49,533	1,964	82	2.38
PO	112	71	36	6,651	237	14	2.14

calls for his defensemen. But Plante's greatest contribution to the art of goaltending was his willingness to roam from the crease, a strategy that he first devised when he was playing in the Quebec junior league during its expansion from four to 11 teams in 1947. "They needed all the players they could get," he explained. "We had four defensemen. One couldn't skate backwards. One couldn't turn to his left. The others were slow. It was a case of me having to go and get the puck when it was shot into our end because our defense couldn't get there fast enough. The more I did it, the farther I went. It seemed to be the best thing to do, so I did it, and it worked."

Despite his success with the powerhouse Canadiens of the 1950s, Plante eventually wore out his welcome in Montreal. The Canadiens faltered three times after five consecutive Stanley Cups, and in 1963, Plante was sent to the Rangers in a trade for Gump Worsley. Plante bragged that he'd win his seventh Vezina Trophy in New York, but playing for such a weak club seemed to cause him to lose heart. Suffering a demotion to the minors, he retired, demoralized, in 1965.

In 1968, however, the St. Louis Blues lured him back to share goaltending duties with Glenn Hall, and the two veterans shared the Vezina Trophy in 1968–69. Rejuvenated, Plante played well into his 40s. Sold to Toronto in 1970, he was dealt to Boston near the end of the 1972–73 campaign, his last in the NHL. Plante had one final stint with Edmonton in the WHA in 1974–75 before retiring for good. He succumbed to cancer in 1986.

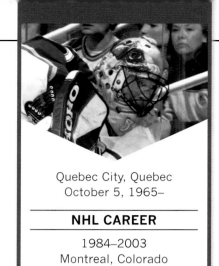

PATRICK ROY

Quebec City, Quebec
October 5, 1965–

NHL CAREER

1984–2003
Montreal, Colorado

Nine goals against in half a game is a goaltender's nightmare, but that ordeal was one of the defining moments of Patrick Roy's career. On December 2, 1995, the Detroit Red Wings sent a relentless barrage of shots at Roy as the Montreal Canadiens put in a particularly hapless effort. Mario Tremblay let Roy twist in the wind in front of a mocking Montreal Forum crowd for far too long. The score was 9–1 before Tremblay gave Roy a merciful hook. Humiliated and enraged, Roy stormed over to Canadiens president Ronald Corey and vehemently declared that he'd played his last game for Montreal. Despite the circumstances, such a public display of insubordination made a trade inevitable. Four days later, Roy was dealt to Colorado.

When the Avalanche faced the Canadiens a few weeks later, Roy was at his best, stopping 37 of 39 shots, for a 5–2 victory. He added a final insult by flipping the puck at Tremblay when the game ended. "It made me feel so good. It was a mistake, but I don't regret it," Roy told the media after the game. "I'm an emotional person. I know sometimes it gets me in trouble, but I know it sometimes helps me to play better too."

The Canadiens were eliminated in the first playoff round that season, but Roy backstopped his team to the Stanley Cup final. The Avalanche won the first two games against the Florida Panthers — Roy let in only a single goal in each game. The Panthers potted two quick goals early in the third game, however, and Roy suffered a barrage of plastic rats from the Florida fans with each goal.

Unlike other goalies who had faced a similar rain of rodents that season, Roy refused to creep back into his net for protection. He skated in small circles as the rats were being scooped up by the maintenance crew, Roy skated over to the Colorado bench. "No more rats," he quietly told his teammates. He did not let in another goal in the series, helping Colorado complete a sweep with a triple overtime shutout in Game 4.

Overtime hockey was nothing new to Roy, who was in goal for the Montreal Canadiens' record-breaking run of 10 consecutive overtime wins in their 1993 Stanley Cup triumph. Those playoff victories cemented his reputation as one of the greatest pressure goalies of all time. Roy was awarded the Conn Smythe Trophy for the second time. It was a feat he had first accomplished as a 20-year-old rookie in the 1985–86 season, the youngest winner ever. "I haven't seen goaltending like that in 14 years," said Larry Robinson at the time, alluding to Ken Dryden's amazing debut. Roy won a record third

AWARDS: 1st All-Star (5), 2nd All-Star (2), Jennings (5), Smythe (3), Vezina (3), Stanley Cup (4), HHOF 2006

STATS:

	GP	W	L	M	GA	SO	AVE
RS	1,029	551	315	60,235	2,546	66	2.54
PO	247	151	94	15,209	584	23	2.30

Smythe after the Avalanche's 2002 Cup victory.

Roy's use of visualization, initially reported as "talking to his goalposts," was a celebrated aspect of his game. While his confidence bordered on arrogance, it was as much a calculated technique as a personality trait. "A goalie has to show he's confident, to his teammates as well as himself," he explained. "You are the last guy before that special red line. You make yourself confident. You make yourself hard to beat."

Roy's style evolved from stand-up to butterfly, best suited to getting his large frame in the way of pucks he couldn't even see. His manner of going down to cover the bottom half of the net became standard practice among young goalies long before Roy decided to retire, at the end of the 2002–03 season, while still at the top of his profession. He left holding the NHL career goaltending records for most games and most wins in both the regular season and the playoffs.

The Avalanche retired Roy's No. 33 in 2003, and in a healing ceremony in 2008 Montreal did the same. "I am reminded tonight of the day in 1984," said Roy, during a speech interrupted by numerous ovations, "when I first put on the noblest suit of armor, the sweater of the Montreal Canadiens. I left a little too soon, without saying goodbye. Tonight, I am coming home."

Winnipeg, Manitoba
December 28, 1929–
May 31, 1970

NHL CAREER

1949–70 Detroit, Boston,
Toronto, Los Angeles,
NY Rangers

TERRY SAWCHUK

Terry Sawchuk's triumphs as a goaltender serve as a counterpoint to his life off the ice. Even his boyhood success was tinged by sadness. His brother died of a heart attack at the age of 17, and 10-year-old Terry inherited his goalie equipment. "The pads were always around the house," Sawchuk explained, "and I fell into them." He was such a natural that he was playing junior hockey within five years and signed his first pro contract with Omaha, in the Detroit Red Wings organization, a few years later.

In the 1950–51 season Sawchuk played all 70 games and had 11 shutouts for the defending Stanley Cup champions in Detroit. He won the Calder Trophy and First All-Star Team honors. The next season he earned a dozen shutouts and won the Vezina Trophy, but he saved the best for last: Detroit swept both 1952 playoff series, and Sawchuk let in only five goals over the eight games for a 0.63 goals-against average.

Sawchuk got his name on the Stanley Cup again in 1954 and 1955. "We could always count on him to come up with the big save," recalled Hockey Hall of Fame defenseman Bob Goldham. "When I look back on those Stanley Cup series, what I remember is 'Ukey' making one big save after another. He was the greatest goaltender who ever lived."

"I try to concentrate on the puck," said Sawchuk, in trying to describe his style. "I'm not a holler guy. I have a very low crouching style; my reflexes are that way, I guess. I can see better through the legs than over some tall guy's shoulder." His vulnerability in placing his face so close to the action wasn't lost on him. "I'm scared every time they get near me," he admitted, and the injuries he sustained over the years — ranging from facial gouges to bone fractures and ruptured spinal disks — are almost incredible. He once quipped: "We are the people who make health insurance popular."

But Sawchuk was loath to miss a game, not wanting to give anyone else a chance to shine. His first NHL break came when he was called up to fill in for Detroit's injured goaltender Harry Lumley.

AWARDS: 1st All-Star (3), 2nd All-Star (4), Calder, Vezina (4), Stanley Cup (4), HHOF 1971

STATS:

	GP	W	L	M	GA	SO	AVE
RS	971	447	330	57,194	2,389	103	2.51
PO	106	54	48	6,290	266	12	2.54

Sawchuk sparkled over a seven-game stint, earning his first of a record 103 career shutouts, and Lumley was traded. After Glenn Hall filled in for Sawchuk for two games in the 1954–55 season, Sawchuk was deemed expendable and traded to the Boston Bruins.

Sawchuk had battled a weight problem over the years, tipping the scales at a portly 230 pounds in 1951 before eventually dropping to a gaunt 170 pounds. His fluttery nerves were typical of those in his profession, but the move to Boston only added to his problems. He quit the game briefly after suffering a nervous collapse. It took a trade back to Detroit in 1957 to get him on track again.

Sawchuk earned All-Star honors twice more in Detroit before the Toronto Maple Leafs picked him up in June 1964. He shared duties with Johnny Bower for three seasons, culminating in Toronto's 1967 upset victories over Chicago and Montreal to win the Stanley Cup. "I'd like to leave hockey like that," said Sawchuk, after an especially outstanding effort against the Black Hawks. "In good style."

It did not happen. "As soon as I go into the net, I bend down and take a sideways peek at the goalposts," Sawchuk once said. "If they look close, I know I'm going to have a good night. Some nights, those damn posts look a mile away." Sawchuk struggled in 1967–68 with Los Angeles, had a disappointing season with Detroit and spent his final year in the NHL being used sparingly

by the New York Rangers. A calamity followed. After engaging in a post-season tussle with a teammate, Sawchuk died in hospital of internal injuries. His induction into the Hockey Hall of Fame in 1971 marked the postscript to a brilliant but tragic career.

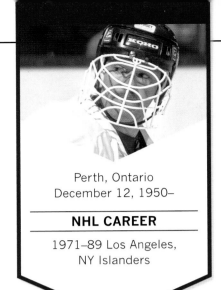

Perth, Ontario
December 12, 1950–

NHL CAREER

1971–89 Los Angeles,
NY Islanders

BILLY SMITH

"I will match them insult for insult," Billy Smith once said — after having given the finger to New York Rangers fans. One of hockey's greatest playoff goalies, "Battlin' Billy" provoked his opponents and their supporters alike. A fierce competitor, he was sometimes known to skip the traditional handshake after losing a playoff series.

"I never saw a goalie so willing to crack people across the ankles with his stick," said Gump Worsley in 1975.

Smith later admitted that he was overly preoccupied with keeping his crease clear of enemy forwards, but rules to protect the goaltender were less stringent at the time than they are today, and the crease was considerably smaller. "I don't bother people unless they're bothering me," he maintained in 1982. "I just try to give myself a little working room. But if a guy bothers me, then I retaliate." But in 1986, he stepped over the line. After breaking the jaw and cheekbone of Chicago's Curt Fraser, he sat out a six-game suspension.

Drafted by Los Angeles in 1970, Smith got only a five-game tryout with the Kings in 1971–72. His future brightened considerably when the New York Islanders picked him up in the 1972 expansion draft. They needed all the help they could get.

Despite playing for a last-place club, Smith showed confidence. Glenn "Chico" Resch became his netminding partner during the 1974–75 season, and the two soon formed one of the NHL's strongest duos. Nervous about overextending himself and getting injured, Smith was content to watch about half of the games from the bench. For the same reason, he avoided on-ice practice as much as possible, concentrating on tennis to enhance his footwork and pioneering the use of computer games and simulations in training to improve his hand-eye coordination.

Smith became the first NHL goalie to score a goal when he made a save against the Colorado Rockies in 1979. With the goaltender pulled during a delayed penalty call, Colorado defenseman Rob Ramage

AWARDS: 1st All-Star, Jennings, Smythe, Vezina, Stanley Cup (4), HHOF 1993

STATS:

	GP	W	L	M	GA	SO	AVE
RS	680	305	233	38,431	2,031	22	3.17
PO	132	88	36	7,645	348	5	2.73

sent an errant pass back to the blue line, only to see it slide all the way into his own net. Smith, the last Islander to have touched the puck, was credited with the goal.

Only once did Smith post a better regular season goals-against average than Resch. "But when it came to the playoffs," said Smith, "I always seemed to get on a roll. There was more pressure, which helped my concentration, and the game seemed a little easier." After several promising seasons, the Islanders won the Stanley Cup four consecutive years starting in 1980, with Smith in the cage for 20 of the 21 playoff games.

"They call [baseball slugger] Reggie Jackson 'Mr. October,'" noted Islanders coach Al Arbour. "'Smitty' is our 'Mr. April' and 'Mr. May.'"

Smith's strong play eventually made Resch expendable. With rookie Roland Melanson as his partner in 1981–82, Smith had his best season. He was selected to the First All-Star Team and received the Vezina Trophy, the first time the NHL's general managers voted for the league's best goalie.

During the 1983 Stanley Cup final, many wondered whether the Islanders' three-year dynasty would crumble before the offensive juggernaut that was the Edmonton Oilers . Not only did Smith meet the Oilers with "probably the finest game I ever played," shutting them out 2–0 in the series opener, but he also denied Wayne Gretzky a single goal in a four-game sweep. Smith was awarded the Conn Smythe Trophy.

The Oilers succeeded in knocking the Islanders off in the next season's final series, and Smith's team went into a rebuilding phase. By then Smith was the last of the original Islanders, though he continued to play effectively until his retirement in 1989. The Islanders retired his No. 31 jersey in 1993, the year Smith was inducted into the Hockey Hall of Fame.

Dmitrovo, Union of Soviet
Socialist Republics
April 25, 1952–

AWARDS

HHOF 1989

VLADISLAV TRETIAK

NHL hockey fans, especially in Canada, waited with glee for the beginning of the 1972 Summit Series. Canada's professionals would finally prove their vast superiority over the Soviet Union, which had been dominating international hockey for a generation with its "amateurs."

While preparing for the first game in Canada, 20-year-old Soviet goaltender Vladislav Tretiak received a surprise visitor, who brought along his own translator. "He meticulously told me, as a goalie, how to play the big Canadian shooters," recalled Tretiak. "Then he shook my hand and left. I can't explain why he came to give me secrets against his own players. Maybe he felt pity that I was so inexperienced, pity for a boy he thought Phil Esposito was going to tear apart. I wish to thank Jacques Plante for his advice."

Team Canada's scouts had reported that Tretiak was the weakest part of his team, but it was the exact opposite. The Canadian goalies detected Plante's influence right away, but the acrobatic Tretiak brought more than insider information to the game. "If there is a comparison to an NHL goalie I would make for Tretiak," remarked Paul Henderson, whose last-minute heroics in the final game gave Canada the narrowest of victories, "it would be Terry Sawchuk."

Over the course of his career, Tretiak won 10 World Championship gold medals, three Olympic golds and one Olympic silver. He was on a record 13 Soviet League Championship teams, selected Soviet Player of the Year five times and won the Gold Stick three times as the season's outstanding European player. These are tremendous achievements, but it was his play against the NHL pros that elevated him to mythic status in North America.

Many still remember the game played in the Montreal Forum on New Year's Eve 1975. Tretiak's Red Army went head-to-head against the Canadiens' dynastic club, backstopped by Ken Dryden. Outshot 38–13, the Soviets earned a 3–3 draw due almost solely to Tretiak's superb play. He was in net when the Soviets beat the NHL All-Stars in the 1979 Challenge Cup, a three-game tournament in Madison Square Garden. In the 1981 Canada Cup tournament, he led his team to victory, allowing only eight goals in six games. "He had better concentration," remarked Wayne Gretzky, "than any goalie I've ever seen."

After picking up clues that Tretiak might be interested in joining them, the Montreal Canadiens selected him in the 1983 NHL entry draft. The Soviet Ice Hockey Federation forbade Tretiak to leave. In the Soviet era, it was not even possible for Tretiak to acknowledge he had

asked for permission. "I would have loved to play in Montreal," he admitted years later, but the dissolution of the Soviet Union came too late for him.

After 15 seasons of playing almost every game for the national team and his own club, Tretiak was burned out. "I reached a point where I got tired of the hockey uniform," he admitted, "and didn't want to put it on anymore." In 1972 he had been given Jacques Plante's book on goaltending. "It seemed to me at that time that he spent too much time on the psychological strains experienced by goalies," said Tretiak. "Now I know how right he was."

Tretiak retired in 1984, only 32 years old. He eventually took an NHL job, as goaltender coach for the Chicago Blackhawks, and he has taught a large number of NHL stars. His No. 20, unheard of as a number for netminders until he made it famous, has been worn in the NHL as a tribute by goalies Ed Belfour, a star pupil, and Evgeni Nabokov, a fellow Russian. Tretiak has received Russia's highest honors in sport, and in 2003 he was elected to the state Duma. In 2006 he was elected head of the Russian Ice Hockey Federation, but he still takes time to teach new generations of goaltenders.

GOALTENDERS
LIONS

Marc-André Fleury............................176
Jaroslav Halak..................................178
Carey Price 180
Jonathan Quick 182
Cam Ward.......................................184

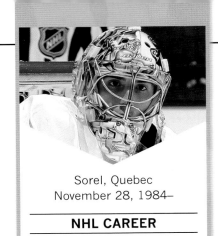

MARC-ANDRÉ FLEURY

Sorel, Quebec
November 28, 1984–

NHL CAREER

2003–
Pittsburgh

Despite his youth, Marc-André Fleury has built a career full of success, disappointment and redemption. He completed three stellar seasons with the Cape Breton Screaming Eagles in the Quebec Major Junior Hockey League, then his dominance at the 2003 World Junior Championship lifted him into the top position at the NHL draft later that year. Although Canada lost the World Junior Championship (WJC) gold medal game 3–2, Fleury was voted the tourney's top goaltender and lauded for keeping his team close. At the NHL draft, with a particularly strong crop of youngsters available, the Pittsburgh Penguins swung a trade with Florida to obtain the first pick overall in order to select the young goalie.

Rumor had it that Pittsburgh co-owner Mario Lemieux strongly encouraged his general manager Craig Patrick to sign Fleury for the 2003–04 season. Lemieux invited the 18-year-old goalie to live with him and his family during Fleury's first NHL training camp; Lemieux remembered how he had felt when he had arrived alone in the city as a French-Canadian teenager. Would he make Fleury pay rent? "Absolutely," laughed Lemieux. "He's got to babysit the kids too. That's what he did last night." (Lemieux made the same offer to his next number-one pick, Sidney Crosby, two years later.)

The Penguins had been in well-publicized financial difficulties for some time, but they opened the vaults for Fleury. On top of the maximum rookie salary, Patrick matched generous incentives the New York Islanders had given their rookie goalie, Rick DiPietro, in 2000, potentially tripling the base salary.

Fleury got off to a strong start in the Pittsburgh net and was the NHL's Rookie of the Month in October 2003 after posting a 2–2–2 record, a 1.96 goals-against average and a 0.943 save percentage. However, the team in front of him was weak, and Fleury began to wither under a heavy barrage of shots. He was determined to stay in the NHL, but Pittsburgh sent him to join Team Canada for the 2004 WJC, seeing the experience as a helpful confidence-booster. The move, however, backfired. Fleury again sparkled for Team Canada, but in the goal medal game against Team U.S.A., with the score tied and less than five minutes to play, Fleury left his net to field a puck and accidentally banked it off a Canadian defenseman into his own net. The miscue held up as the difference, and Fleury returned with another silver medal and, in the eyes of rabid Canadian hockey fans, a pair of goat horns.

After only a handful of games back in Pittsburgh, Fleury was sent to Cape Breton, where he finished out the season, and then to the American Hockey League's Wilkes-Barre/Scranton Penguins. He remained in the AHL through the NHL lockout of 2004–05 and for the start of the 2005–06 campaign, but by the end of the season he had settled in as Pittsburgh's starting goalie. He signed a contract extension with the Penguins in August 2006 for a relatively modest $2.59 million over two years.

The Penguins made the playoffs for the first time in four seasons during the 2006–07 campaign, and the next year Fleury posted a stellar 0.933 save percentage in the playoffs, backstopping the Penguins all the way to the 2008 Stanley Cup final. Unfortunately, with his team's back to the wall in the sixth game against Detroit, Fleury tried to cover a puck and accidentally knocked it backward into his own net. Again, an error held up as the winning goal.

The Penguins showed complete faith in Fleury with a seven-year $35-million contract extension the following summer, and he played a significant role in getting the Penguins back to the Cup final in the spring of 2009. Once again facing the powerful Detroit squad, Fleury and the Penguins looked overmatched on paper, yet they managed to split the first four games. In the fifth game, a 5–0 Detroit win, Fleury got the hook in the second period, but he rebounded strongly in Game 6, and Pittsburgh eked out a 2–1 victory. In the deciding seventh game, Fleury was again at his best. A diving save against a hard shot by Detroit's Nicklas Lidstrom with two seconds remaining defined his outstanding performance, and he preserved Pittsburgh's 2–1 lead and hoisted the Stanley Cup.

A star in the present and a goalie for the future, he earned a gold medal as the third-string backup for Team Canada at the 2010 Olympics, but we will undoubtedly see Fleury shining on hockey's main stages for years to come.

AWARDS: Stanley Cup

STATS:

	GP	W	L	M	GA	SO	AVE
RS	367	184	126	20,859	951	19	2.74
PO	69	41	28	4,188	176	5	2.52

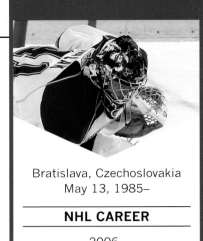

Bratislava, Czechoslovakia
May 13, 1985–

NHL CAREER

2006–
Montreal, St. Louis

JAROSLAV HALAK

In spring 2010, Jaroslav Halak had Montreal Canadiens fans recalling the goaltending exploits of franchise legends Ken Dryden and Patrick Roy. A month later, those same fans were shocked and dismayed when their playoff hero was traded to St. Louis for a couple of prospects. Such is the life of a goalie in today's NHL.

Halak was born in present-day Slovakia, a country better known for goal-scorers than netminders, where he played junior hockey from 2001 to 2004. Picked late in the 2003 NHL entry draft by the Canadiens (9th round, 271st pick), Halak began to work with Montreal's goalie coach at the time.

"[Rollie Melanson] was the big key for me," Halak told *InGoal Magazine*'s Kevin Woodley in 2010. "He really helped me a lot to develop my system and I am just trying to maintain the same things he taught me."

In 2004–05, Halak joined the Lewiston Maineiacs in the Quebec Major Junior Hockey League. He started the 2005–06 season with the Long Beach Ice Dogs of the ECHL before earning a promotion to the Hamilton Bulldogs of the American Hockey League (AHL). By the 2006–07 campaign, he was an AHL star, leading the league in goals-against average. On February 18, 2007, Halak played his first game for the

Canadiens and notched his first NHL shutout just over a month later. Although he started the following campaign back with the Bulldogs, he was back in Montreal in February 2008, when Cristobal Huet was traded.

Carey Price had been anointed starting goalie, but Halak played in 34 games for Montreal in 2008–09. When Price faltered the following season, Halak stepped firmly into the breach and posted 26 wins against 13 losses. At the 2010 Olympics, he bolstered his reputation as Slovakia's netminder. Wearing a mask that honored Vladimir Dzurilla, Slovakia's goaltending hero of the 1970s, and Juraj Janosik, a famous 17th-century Slovak folk hero who always fought for the underdog, Halak backstopped Slovakia to a fourth-place finish, the country's best Olympic hockey result ever.

After helping Montreal scrape into the 2010 playoffs with 88 points, Halak was named the Canadiens' starter, over Carey Price, against the powerhouse Washington Capitals, who had led the league with 121 points. After a surprise 3–2 overtime win in the series opener, Halak lost the second game in overtime, and he was then pulled in the second period of a Game 3 loss. Price lost Game 4, and with his team facing elimination, Halak got the start for Game 5.

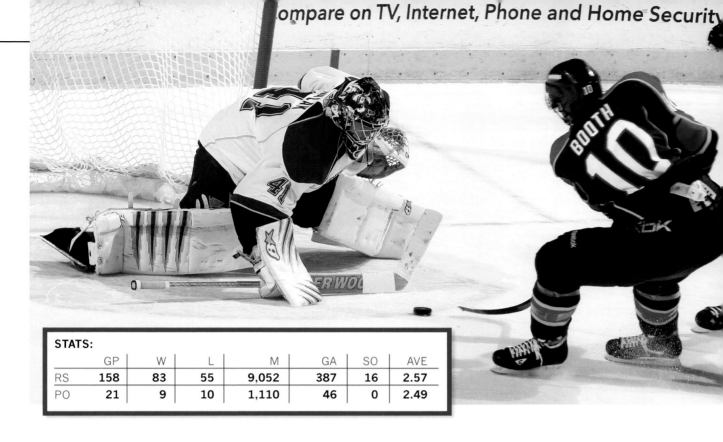

STATS:	GP	W	L	M	GA	SO	AVE
RS	158	83	55	9,052	387	16	2.57
PO	21	9	10	1,110	46	0	2.49

"Everybody knew what kind of game we needed to play and we did it," said Halak, who made 37 saves to help Montreal eke out a 2–1 victory. "But still, we're trailing by one and it's still do-or-die for us. We need to play our best all the time now."

True to his word and in spectacular form, Halak was close to perfection in the next game, stopping 53 shots (a regulation-time club record) en route to a 4–1 Montreal win.

"I think we played great and we just didn't score," said Washington sniper Alex Ovechkin. "It's only one guy…. He [did] an unbelievable job. What more can you say?"

"Another day in the office," quipped Halak, who was again the difference in the deciding seventh game. Outshot 42–16, Montreal won 2–1 to move on to face Pittsburgh, the defending Stanley Cup champion. In the opening game, Halak appeared tired and left early in the third period, with Montreal down 5–2. But he responded in the second game, making 38 saves in a 3–1 victory. "I needed to be better, I knew that," said Halak.

He held Pittsburgh scoreless into the third period of Game 3, but the Canadiens eventually lost 2–0. He then backstopped Montreal to a 3–2 win in Game 4 to even the series. The Penguins took a 3–2 series lead after Game 5, yet Montreal pushed them to a seventh game, despite being outshot 37–25 in Game 6. Halak stole the show again in Game 7, with the shots 39–20 in Pittsburgh's favor, and the Canadiens went to the conference final for the first time since winning the Cup in 1993. Montreal succumbed to Philadelphia in just five games. Halak was hailed as a hero, but he was nonetheless traded to St. Louis.

Halak described his years in Montreal as "a real nice memory, but that's in the past."

He got his 2010–11 campaign with St. Louis off to a roaring start. Clearly the No. 1 goalie for the first time in his NHL career, and with a new four-year $15-million contract freshly signed, he maintains an even keel. "You won't stop all the pucks every night," he said. "The only thing you can do is bring your best every time you play."

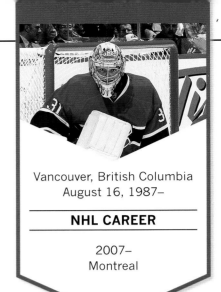

CAREY PRICE

Vancouver, British Columbia
August 16, 1987–

NHL CAREER

2007–
Montreal

In 2006–07, Carey Price added an unprecedented treasure trove to his trophy case. He backstopped Canada to a gold medal at the World Junior Championship and was voted the tournament's top goalie and MVP. With his Western Hockey League (WHL) junior team, the Tri-City Americans, he earned the league's Goaltender of the Year title and First All-Star Team status, as well as the Canadian League Goaltender of the Year award.

Price immediately launched his professional career, joining the Hamilton Bulldogs of the American League for the last three games of their season as well as the ensuing playoffs. Backstopping the Bulldogs to the league title, Price, still a teenager, became the youngest player ever to win the AHL's Jack A. Butterfield Trophy as playoff MVP.

Price's roots may have been small-town British Columbia (his mother was once chief of the Ulkatcho First Nation), but none of this glory was completely unexpected. Montreal chose Price with their first pick (fifth overall) in the 2005 entry draft, based on his stellar play in the WHL. After his successes the following season, the Canadiens promoted Price to the NHL for the 2007–08 season. Although he was still only 20 years old, he assumed the starter's role when

Cristobal Huet was traded in March 2008. Price led all rookie goalies, with 24 wins, a 0.920 save percentage and three shutouts, then notched two more blanks in the playoffs.

Agile and quick, Price seemed almost unflappable, and he was voted the starting goalie for the 2009 All-Star Game in Montreal. But the Canadiens barely made the playoffs and then exited them quickly. When the Canadiens fans razzed Price after he gave up four goals in two periods of what proved to be the final game in a four-game sweep by Boston, the young goaltender raised his arms in an angry and highly public protest.

Price struggled for most of the 2009–10 season, with his last start of the campaign pretty much summing up his year. After losing his starting position to Jaroslav Halak late in the season, Price had relieved his usurper in the middle of the third game of a first-round playoff series against the top-ranked Washington Capitals and earned the start for the fourth game. But when the tide of the latter game turned Washington's way with two quick goals midway through the third period, putting the Capitals ahead 4–2, Price fired the puck at the celebrating Washington players. He missed them but picked up an unsportsmanlike conduct penalty. The Canadiens pulled Price with

STATS:

	GP	W	L	M	GA	SO	AVE
RS	206	98	76	12,013	520	12	2.60
PO	26	8	14	1,457	69	3	2.84

almost three minutes left in the game, and the Capitals potted an empty-netter. Montreal again got within two goals with a minute and a half left in the game, but Washington put another puck into the vacant Montreal net. Down 6–3 and with only 11 seconds on the clock, Price came off the bench and swung his stick angrily toward the last Washington goal-scorer, Nicklas Backstrom, and got his second unsportsmanlike conduct penalty.

"It's frustration," said Price after the game. "That's part of hockey." Quoting Paul Newman's character in the movie *Slapshot*, he added, "Let 'em know you're there."

But Halak got the remaining starts that season, brilliantly leading Montreal to upsets of the Capitals and Pittsburgh before falling to Philadelphia. Halak and Price were both restricted free agents, and the public consensus seemed to be that Halak was now No. 1. The Canadiens' braintrust, however, had a different opinion and quickly traded Halak to St. Louis, unequivocally staking their future with Price, the younger of the two goalies by two years.

In 2010–11 Price justified his backers' faith in him. "When I was sitting on the bench there was a decision that I made," said Price. "If things weren't going to work out, it wasn't going to be from a lack of effort."

Although he wasn't even listed with the 18 goalies on the NHL's All-Star Game ballot for fan voting, Price received the second-most votes as a write-in candidate and played in the mid-season exhibition. "It's a nice reward," said Price, "But obviously the real reward is at the end of the season."

Price will ultimately be judged on how he performs for Montreal at that critical part of the year, but he appears poised to solidify the Canadiens crease for years to come.

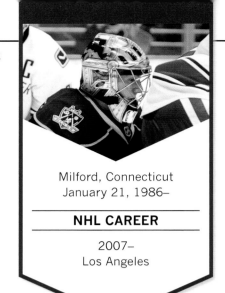

Milford, Connecticut
January 21, 1986–

NHL CAREER

2007–
Los Angeles

JONATHAN QUICK

His surname is appropriate, but Jonathan Quick's natural athleticism and outstanding flexibility are the keys to his success. Although not overly large, at 6-foot-1 and about 210 pounds, he can cover the entire bottom of the net with the splits, keeping both pads on the ice.

He showed early promise as a New England prep school star with the storied Avon Old Farms in his home state of Connecticut. Quick backstopped his team to consecutive high school championships, going 27–1 as a junior and 25–2 as a senior. The Los Angeles Kings selected him in the third round of the 2005 NHL entry draft (72nd overall). Colleges also came calling in 2005, and Quick accepted a scholarship from the University of Massachusetts.

In his second season with the UMass Minutemen, Quick helped the team get to its first ever NCAA championship, in the spring of 2007. He was named a Second Team All-American in the Hockey East conference then decided it was time to leave academic life to pursue the professional game. Hoping to make enough of an impression in Los Angeles to stick with the Kings after the 2007–08 training camp, Quick instead found himself riding the bus with the Reading Royals in the East Coast Hockey League.

"I saw a lot of pucks … and learned a lot," he recalled. He notched 23 wins and three ties in 38 appearances and earned a promotion to the American Hockey League. With the Manchester Monarchs, Quick only went 11–8 over the remainder of the season, but his 0.922 save percentage and 2.32 goals-against average were both stellar. Quick also got into his first NHL action that season, appearing in three games after the Kings' starting goalie was injured.

He started the 2008–09 campaign back with Manchester, but in December got the call-up he'd been working toward. Quick had his first NHL shutout during his first week, and by season's end he had established himself as the Kings' number-one goalie. Over 44 appearances, he tallied 21 wins while losing in overtime twice and four times in a shootout. Over one remarkable three-game stretch, he earned the NHL's First Star of the Week honors when he stopped 95 of 100 shots, notching three road victories. At season's end, his 2.48 goals-against average and 0.914 save percentage were solid numbers for a goalie on a team that finished last in its division, well out of the playoffs.

Quick not only had the honor of being the third goalie on Team U.S.A. at the 2010 Olympics, his entire 2009–10 season went well. He set Los Angeles team records for most games played (72) and most wins (39), and the Kings made the playoffs for the first time in six seasons. Facing the powerhouse Vancouver Canucks, Quick stopped 41 of 44 shots in the opening game, but the Kings lost in overtime. While the Kings then took a surprising 2–1 lead in the series, Vancouver successfully wore them down in the end, winning the series 4–2. "The team played great," Quick told Rich Hammond of lakingsinsider.com. "They battled hard all series. That's a very good Canucks team over there. We played well for six games. Obviously it's not the outcome we wanted, but we've got some time to reflect on the season and start getting ready for next year."

Quick faced some strong competition in his 2010–11 training camp from Jonathan Bernier, a highly touted prospect whom Quick had played with briefly in Manchester. Many forecasters predicted Bernier would get the nod and possibly make Quick expendable. However, Quick not only retained the starting position, he further endeared himself to his club by maintaining his team-first attitude. "It might look like I'm getting a lot of work," he said modestly after an early-season game against the New Jersey Devils, when his team was outshot 40–23 yet won 3–1. "But a lot of them were from the perimeter and I was able to see a ton of them. The guys did a great job of picking up guys and clearing out lanes. The ones I wasn't able to control, they were able to get the rebounds and get them to the corners. So it was a great team effort."

He might not be the one saying it, but Quick deserves a lot of credit for LA becoming one of hockey's best young teams.

STATS:

	GP	W	L	M	GA	SO	AVE
RS	180	96	66	10,485	426	14	2.44
PO	12	4	5	740	41	1	3.32

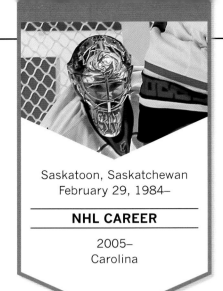

Saskatoon, Saskatchewan
February 29, 1984–

NHL CAREER

2005–
Carolina

CAM WARD

While he had paid some dues, it was an unexpected turn of events when rookie goaltender Cam Ward got the opportunity to star in the 2006 Stanley Cup playoffs. He had established himself as a capable, but not spectacular, backup to Martin Gerber on the Carolina Hurricanes. In 28 games over the regular season, he had earned 14 wins while posting a 0.882 save percentage and a 3.68 goals-against average, his worst season totals to date. Gerber had vastly superior numbers, but when he faltered and Carolina, which had tied for third overall in the NHL over the regular season, looked like it was about to lose its second playoff game against the underdog Montreal Canadiens, Ward got the call.

Although Ward lost that second game in overtime, he helped the Canes vanquish the Canadiens with four straight wins then backstopped Carolina to a 4–1 series victory over his childhood hero Martin Brodeur and the New Jersey Devils in the second round. He then outdueled highly heralded rookie goalie Ryan Miller and the Buffalo Sabres in a seven-game Eastern Conference final, giving Carolina a chance to face the Edmonton Oilers for the Stanley Cup.

Although he was born in Saskatchewan, Ward had grown up cheering for the Oilers, living just outside Edmonton in Sherwood Park, Alberta. He was the Western Hockey League's Rookie of the Year in 2001–02, during his first of three junior seasons with the Red Deer Rebels. The Hurricanes selected him with their first pick, 25th overall, in the 2002 NHL draft.

He graduated to the Lowell Lock Monsters in the American Hockey League in 2004–05 and made the AHL's All-Rookie Team, so by 2006 one could have argued that he had earned his shot when he entered the Carolina net with hockey's biggest prize at stake. But this was rarified air, and Ward was the first rookie goalie to start a Stanley Cup playoff game, post a shutout and win a Stanley Cup ring since Patrick Roy had accomplished that trifecta 20 years earlier.

The Canes nearly beat the Oilers in five games, losing a heartbreaker in overtime. They were then pushed to a seventh game, but Ward only let in a single goal as Carolina won 3–1 on home ice. Ward was awarded the Conn Smythe Trophy as most valuable player of the playoffs, and the state of North Carolina had its first major league championship in any sport.

After winning the Cup, the Canes seemed hungover for most of the following season and didn't even qualify for the playoffs. Ward got a strong measure of redemption when he joined

AWARDS: Smythe, Stanley Cup

STATS:

	GP	W	L	M	GA	SO	AVE
RS	346	175	126	19,733	901	16	2.74
PO	41	23	18	2,421	96	4	2.38

Team Canada at the 2007 World Championship, winning all five games he started, including the final match, to earn a gold medal. But he had finished well below the NHL elite in goals-against average and save percentage in 2006–07. He took that to heart and arrived at Carolina's 2007–08 training camp having shed 25 pounds in the off-season. "I worked hard this summer and got myself probably in the best shape I've ever been in my entire life," Ward told the Canadian Press, noting his weight was one area the coaching staff indicated needed some attention. Noticeably slimmer and quicker, Ward also admitted he had heard those who questioned whether his Conn Smythe Trophy win had been a fluke. "People are going to have their opinions, but I know what I'm

capable of doing," said Ward. "It's just a matter of going out there and playing to the best of my capability.… I'm doing the best I can to get myself not only physically but mentally prepared each and every night and not let one game slip by."

The Hurricanes, however, failed to reach the post-season again. Ward helped Canada try to defend its World Championship gold, losing the final game in overtime. In 2008–09, he tasted more playoff success, helping Carolina to the Eastern Conference final. Ward was one of the busiest and best goalies in 2010–11, making over 2,000 saves for the Canes. At the 2011 NHL All-Star Game, with a new format to generate more fan interest, his Hurricanes teammate Eric Staal had the first pick in choosing sides. "I'm going to take my boy, Cam Ward," smiled Staal, to absolutely no one's surprise.

ACKNOWLEDGEMENTS

The idea behind *Hockey's Greatest Stars: Legends and Young Lions* evolved from conversations with Lionel Koffler and Michael Worek of Firefly Books. Their colleague Steve Cameron subsequently steered this volume to completion with diligent care and patience. Lawrence Scanlan was of immense help in shaping my original manuscript, as were Tracy Read and Susan Dickinson of Bookmakers Press. Special thanks on this edition is also extended to Sarah Jane Dawson of Firefly Books and designer Kimberley Young.

I appreciate the support of my colleagues Bryan Lavery and Kathy McLaughlin, who enabled me to spend time on this book, as well as the wide group of friends who served as a helpful sounding board. I am indebted to Jane Antoniak for her research and suggestions for a number of the new player profiles in this edition, as well as my daughter and historian Tara McDonell-Gordon, who assisted with research on some profiles and compiled much of the statistical data.

The rest of my family also continues to be a support, especially my parents, Alanson and Nora McDonell, as well as my siblings, in-laws and an extensive clan. I am thankful for my sons Quinn and Isaac McDonell-Gordon and daughter Tara, who remain consistently enthusiastic boosters of my writing career. My biggest appreciation is for the loving care of my partner and soul mate, Sue Gordon, who retains her enthusiasm for life through all obstacles, and strengthens me in immeasurable ways.

DEDICATION

To Sue Gordon, for her faith in me, and to Isaac, Tara and Quinn McDonell-Gordon, with love and affection.

PHOTO CREDITS

BIBLIOGRAPHY

The books listed here were of immeasurable assistance, but several other sources were equally useful. The archived newspaper and magazine clippings at the Hockey Hall of Fame in Toronto as well as the Hall web site (www.hhof.com) provided a wealth of material. Other internet sites I frequently visited are run by the NHL (www.nhl.com), the *Sun* newspaper chain (www.canoe.com/Hockey/home. html); ESPN (ESPNET.SportsZone.com/nhl); and LCS Guide to Hockey. (www.lcshockey.com), written by Joe Pelletier and Pat Houda. Dozens of other web sites — primarily run by fans out of an enthusiastic loyalty to the game and particular players — were of some practical use. Many newspaper web sites, especially those of *The Boston Globe*, *The St. Louis Post-Dispatch*, *The London Free Press*, *The Toronto Star*, and *The Globe and Mail* were also helpful.

Dozens of issues of *The Hockey News* were used as sources, and their numerous writers and editors deserve credit, not only from me, for the fine work they do for the sport of hockey. Articles in *Sports Illustrated* were also useful. Several editions of the annual *National Hockey League Official Guide and Record Book* and both volumes of *Total Hockey: The Official Encyclopedia of the National Hockey League* were indispensable for their statistical information, as were a large assortment of individual clubs' NHL media guides.

Benedict, Michael, and D'Arcy Jenish, eds. *Canada On Ice: Fifty Years of Great Hockey.* Toronto: The Penguin Group, 1998.

Brewitt, Ross. *Last Minute of Play: Tales of Hockey Grit and Glory.* Toronto: Stoddart Publishing Co. Ltd., 1993.

Dryden, Steve, ed. *The Top 100: NHL Players of All Time.* Toronto: McClelland & Stewart Inc., 1998.

Fischler, Stan. *Bad Boys: The Legends of Hockey's Toughest, Meanest, Most-Feared Players.* Whitby: McGraw-Hill Ryerson Ltd, 1991.

-------- . *Bobby Orr and the Big, Bad Bruins.* New York: Dell Publishing Co., Inc., 1969.

-------- . *Golden Ice: The Greatest Teams in Hockey History.* Scarborough: McGraw-Hill Ryerson Ltd., 1990.

-------- . *The Rivalry: Canadiens vs Leafs.* Whitby: McGraw-Hill Ryerson Ltd, 1991.

Goyens, Chris and Allan Turowetz. *Lions in Winter.* Scarborough: Prentice-Hall Canada Inc., 1986.

Houston, William. *Pride & Glory: 100 Years of the Stanley Cup.* Whitby: McGraw-Hill Ryerson Ltd., 1992.

Hughes, Morgan. *Best of Hockey.* Chicago: Publications International, Inc., 1998.

-------- . *Hockey Legends of All Time.* Chicago: Publications International, Inc., 1996.

Hunter, Douglas. *A Breed Apart: An Illustrated History of Goaltending.* Toronto: Viking, 1995.

-------- . *Champions: The Illustrated History of Hockey's Greatest Dynasties.* Toronto: Penguin Studio, 1997.

-------- . *Open Ice: The Tim Horton Story.* Toronto: Viking, 1997.

Irvin, Dick. *The Habs: An Oral History of the Montreal Canadiens, 1940-1980.* Toronto: McClelland & Stewart, 1991.

Klein, Jeff Z. and Karl-Eric Reif. *The Coolest Guys on Ice.* Atlanta: Turner Publishing, Inc., 1996.

Leonetti, Mike. *Hockey's Golden Era: Stars of the Original Six.* Toronto: Macmillan of Canada, 1993.

MacGregor, Roy. *The Home Team: Fathers, Sons & Hockey.* Toronto: Viking, 1995.

McDonell, Chris. *For the Love of Hockey: Hockey Stars' Personal Stories.* Richmond Hill: Firefly Books Ltd., 1997.

McKinley, Michael. *Hockey Hall of Fame Legends.* Toronto: Viking/Opus Productions, 1993.

Potvin, Denis with Stan Fischler. *Power On Ice.* New York, Harper & Row, 1977.

Robinson, Larry and Chris Goyens. *Robinson For the Defence.* Scarborough: McGraw-Hill Ryerson Ltd., 1988.

Romain, Joseph and James Duplacey. *Hockey Superstars.* Toronto: Smithbooks in Canada, 1994.

Roxborough, Henry. *The Stanley Cup Story.* Toronto: The Ryerson Press, 1964.

INDEX

Abel, Sid, 66, 78, 114
Adams, Jack, 58, 66, 148, 158
Apps, Syl, 12–13
Arbour, Al, 125, 171

Babcock, Mike, 116
Backstrom, Nicklas, 44–45, 181
Bailey, Ace, 60, 128, 129
Ballard, Harold, 112
Bathgate, Andy, 64, 80, 164
Bauer, Bobby, 34
Belfour, Ed, 160, 173
Beliveau, Jean, 14–15, 33, 76
Benedict, Clint, 104
Bettman, Gary, 85
Blake, Toe, 32, 33, 82, 164
Boivin, Leo, 124
Bossy, Mike, 38, 56–57, 84
Bouchard, Butch, 34
Boudreau, Bruce, 90
Bourdon, Lou, 136
Bourque, Raymond, 100–101
Bower, Johnny, 144–145, 169
Bowman, Scotty, 116, 152
Brimsek, Frank, 146–147
Broda, Turk, 148–149
Brodeur, Martin, 150–151, 159, 184
Bucyk, John, 58–59
Bure, Pavel, 9, 116
Burke, Brian, 92
Bylsma, Dan, 49

Calder, Frank, 105, 107
Campbell, Brian, 88, 90
Campbell, Clarence, 84, 107
Carlyle, Randy, 93
Carson, Jimmy, 51
centers, 10–53
    legends, 10–41
    lions, 42–53
Chadwick, Ed, 144
Chelios, Chris, 102–103
Chelios, Gus, 102
Cherry, Don, 120, 126
Chretien, Jean, 81
Christie, James, 14
Clancy, King, 30, 60, 104–105, 112
Clapper, Dit, 106–107, 146
Clarke, Bobby, 16–17, 74
Coffey, Paul, 108–109, 134
Cole, Erik, 133

Conacher, Charlie, 8, 60–61, 64
Conacher, Pete, 61
Conacher, Roy, 61
Cook, Bun, 30
Corbeau, Bert, 36
Cowley, Bill, 107
Crosby, Sidney, 25, 46–47, 48, 49, 51, 53, 90, 92, 176

Dandurand, Leo, 30
Day, Hap, 64
defensemen, 98–141
    legends, 98–129
    lions, 130–141
Delvecchio, Alex, 81
Dionne, Marcel, 9, 18–19, 22
DiPietro, Rick, 176
Doughty, Drew, 132–133, 140
Douglas, Kent, 129
Dryden, Dave, 152
Dryden, Ken, 152–153, 166, 178
Dumart, Woody, 34
Durnan, Bill, 154–155
Dzurilla, Vladimir, 178

Eagleson, Alan, 119
Eaton, Mark, 90
Eddolls, Frank, 122
Emms, Hap, 162
Esposito, Phil, 9, 18, 20–21, 35, 100, 172
Esposito, Tony, 9

Faulkner, Steve, 154
Favell, Doug, 162
Fleury, Marc-André, 46, 176–177
Forsberg, Peter, 44
Francis, Emile, 120
Franzen, Johan, 44
Fuhr, Grant, 156–157

Gadsby, Bill, 112
Gagner, Sam, 89
Gartner, Mike, 9, 62–63
Geoffrion, Bernie, 64–65, 69
Getzlaf, Ryan, 93, 95
Gillies, Clark, 56
goaltenders, 142–187
    legends, 142–173
    lions, 174–185
Goldham, Bob, 168
Gonchar, Sergei, 48, 136
Green, Mike, 134–135

Gretzky, Wayne, 9, 18, 19, 21, 22–23, 24, 26, 40, 46, 49, 51, 67, 70, 74, 75, 91, 108, 132, 160
Gzowski, Peter, 80

Halak, Jaroslav, 178–179
Hall, Glenn, 79, 158–159
Hanlon, Glen, 134
Hart, Cecil, 30, 31
Harvey, Doug, 110–111
Hasek, Dominik, 156, 160–161
Henderson, Paul, 9, 20
Hextall, Ron, 151
Hitchman, Lionel, 106
Hodge, Ken, 20, 35
Horner, Red, 128
Horton, Lori, 112
Horton, Tim, 112–113
Howe, Gordie, 8, 21, 62, 64, 66–67, 80, 81, 103, 106, 119, 123, 128
Howe, Mark, 68
Howe, Marty, 68
Hull, Bobby, 20, 21, 22, 29, 68–69
Hull, Brett, 70–71

Imlach, Punch, 112, 144
Irvin, Dick, 34
Ivan, Tommy, 123

Jackson, Harvey, 60
Jackson, Reggie, 171
Jagr, Jaromir, 72–73
Joliat, Aurèle, 31

Kane, Patrick, 52, 88–89
Keenan, Mike, 71
Kelly, Red, 16, 28, 113, 114–115
Kennedy, Ted, 66
Kharlamov, Valeri, 16
Kiszka, Frank, 102
Koivu, Mikko, 95
Kostitsyn, Sergei, 89
Kurri, Jari, 74–75

Lafleur, Guy, 9, 18, 38, 76–77, 91, 126, 127
Laich, Brooks, 45
Lapointe, Guy, 126
Leach, Reggie, 75
Lemaire, Jacques, 77
Lemieux, Mario, 24–25, 40, 46, 48, 49, 72, 108, 109, 134, 176
Leonsis, Ted, 90
Letang, Kris, 136–137
Lidstrom, Nicklas, 116–117
Linden, Trevor, 160
Lindsay, Ted, 66, 78–79, 110, 158

Lumley, Harry, 168

MacGregor, Roy, 38
MacNeil, Al, 32
Mahovlich, Frank, 80–81, 114
Malkin, Evgeni, 46, 48–49
Marotte, Gilles, 20
Martin, Paul, 136
Martin, Pit, 20
Martin, Rick, 56
McDonald, Bucko, 118
McKenzie, Bob, 132
McNeil, Gerry, 155
McPhee, George, 45, 97
Melanson, Roland, 171, 178
Melrose, Barry, 50
Messier, Mark, 26–27, 62, 156
Mikita, Stan, 21, 28–29, 69
Mohns, Doug, 28
Moog, Andy, 156, 157
Moore, Dickie, 82–83
Morenz, Howie, 8, 30–31
Morrow, Brenden, 93
Mowers, Johnny, 146
Murphy, Larry, 63
Murray, Bob, 92
Myers, Tyler, 140

Nabokov, Evgeni, 173
Nicholson, Bob, 47
Niemi, Antti, 88
Nighbor, Frank, 104
Norris, Jack, 20
Nylander, Michael, 44

Oates, Adam, 70
Orpik, Brooks, 90
Orr, Bobby, 18, 21, 22, 58, 108, 116, 118–119, 120, 124, 125, 132, 133
Orr, Doug, 118
Osgood, Chris, 161
Ovechkin, Alex, 44, 46, 48, 90–91, 96, 134

Pang, Darren, 156
Parent, Bernie, 17, 162–163
Park, Brad, 21, 120–121
Patrick, Lynn, 35
Perry, Corey, 92–93, 95
Picard, Noel, 119
Pilote, Pierre, 122–123
Plante, Jacques, 164–165, 172, 173
Pocklington, Peter, 22, 108
Poile, David, 141
Potvin, Denis, 121, 124–125
Potvin, Felix, 156

Potvin, Jean, 124
Pratt, Babe, 123
Price, Carey, 178, 180–181
Primeau, Joe, 60
Puck, Peter, 108

Quackenbush, Bill, 12
Quick, Jonathan, 182–183

Ranford, Bill, 157
Ratelle, Jean, 21, 120
Rayner, Chuck, 144
Resch, Glenn, 170
Richard, Henri, 32–33, 82
Richard, Maurice, 32, 33, 37, 56, 64, 69, 84–85, 147
Roberts, Gary, 51
Roberts, Gordie, 72
Robinson, Larry, 109, 126–127, 166
Rollins, Al, 149
Ross, Art, 107, 147
Roy, Patrick, 151, 166–167, 178
Ruff, Lindy, 160
Ryan, Bobby, 94–95
Ryan, Shane, 94

Sakic, Joe, 101, 132
Salming, Borje, 116
Sanderson, Derek, 112, 119
Sather, Glen, 22, 108
Savard, Serge, 126
Sawchuk, Terry, 58, 145, 150, 168–169
Schenn, Luke, 140
Schmidt, Milt, 34–35, 162
Selke, Frank, 114
Semin, Alexander, 96–97
Shanahan, Brendan, 8
Shero, Ray, 51
Shore, Eddie, 30, 104, 106, 118, 119, 128–129
Shultz, Dave, 126
Siebert, Babe, 36
Simmer, Charlie, 19
Simmons, Don, 129
Simpson, Craig, 26
Sinden, Harry, 118
Smith, Billy, 170–171

Smith, Hooley, 36
Smyth, Ryan, 133
Smythe, Conn, 12, 60, 148, 149
Staal, Eric, 185
Staal, Jordan, 46
Stamkos, Steven, 50–51
Stanfield, Fred, 20, 35
Stevenson, Melody, 94
Stevenson, Robert, 94
Stewart, Jacks, 35
Stewart, Nels, 8, 36–37, 84
Sundin, Mats, 160
Suter, Bob, 138
Suter, Gary, 138
Suter, John, 138
Suter, Ryan, 138–139, 141

Taylor, Dave, 19
Thompson, Tiny, 146
Titanic, Paul, 50
Tkachuk, Keith, 45
Toews, Jonathan, 46, 52–53, 88, 89
Tremblay, Mario, 166
Tretiak, Vladislav, 9, 172–173
Trottier, Bryan, 38–39, 41, 56

Vadnais, Carol, 21
Vezina, Georges, 8

Ward, Cam, 184–185
Watson, Harry, 13
Weber, Shea, 140–141
Weir, Trevor, 50
Wharram, Ken, 28
Wilson, Johnny, 38
wingers, 54–97
    legends, 54–85
    lions, 86–97
Worsley, Gump, 33, 69, 144, 165, 170

Yzerman, Steve, 8, 40–41, 117

Zanussi, Joe, 21, 120
Zetterberg, Henrik, 44, 47